Advance

Electronic addiction is a real problem for kids and teens today. Dr. Jay Berk beautifully addresses this delicate subject matter in his easy to read, practical book, making it invaluable to parents who want to help their children combat this problem. Full of expert advice, wisdom and a wealth of helpful suggestions, this is a must read for every parent who has a child living in today's world.

~ Denise Simon, author of *Parenting in the Spotlight: How to Raise a Child Star without Screwing Them Up*

The target audience of Dr. Jay Berk's book, *Parent's Quick Guide to Electronic Addiction*, is parents of children old enough to use any electronic media, from toddlers to late adolescents. However, it could have easily been titled *Quick Guide to Electronic Addiction...* period. Readers of all ages will easily recognize themselves and their need to "recover" from the domination of electronic media in their lives, from video gaming to smartphone enslavement. Dr. Berk paints a vivid portrait of how our culture is confronted by new addiction no less damaging to our well-being than alcohol, drugs, and substance addiction.

In layman's terms, he provides clear and convincing evidence of how and why the use of electronic media has insidiously captured the minds of our children and held them hostage from friends, family, and the joys of meaningful living. He graphically describes how electronic addiction can capture our children at every developmental stage and shares addiction symptoms that can be easily spotted by minimally alert parents.

While Dr. Berk leaves no stones unturned in laying out the case for electronic addiction in our children in clear and compelling terms, he details the ransom parents must pay to free their children. In real-world language he presents an irrefutable case for strong parenting, but also offers parents detailed strategies ranging from guidance for early childhood training to supportive intervention for older children. He leaves no doubt there is a ransom for freeing our children, but concludes, "the result is a child who can use electronics in a safe and healthy way while maintaining positive relationships in the real world." The ransom presented is planning, compassionate parenting, and support from "the village" of adults in a child's life. In simple and direct terms, Dr. Berk places these powerful tools in a parent's hands and provides expert guidance in their use.

Kudos to Dr. Berk for his insight, compassion, and thoughtful tools to support parents in reuniting with their children on the other side of this crippling addiction. BUT, whether you are a parent of a child captured by this addiction or an adult who is aware that you are "not there" for family and friends because of your own electronic addiction, this book is for you. The sooner you buy it, the sooner you, too, can be released.

~ Raymond Akridge, President, Education Leadership, Inc.

Parent's Quick Guide to Electronic Addiction

Jay Berk, Ph.D

Wilmington, DE

Author Contact: CenterforElectronicAddiction.com

Thomas Noble Books

Wilmington, DE

www.thomasnoblebooks.com

Library of Congress Control Number: 2018936804

ISBN: 978-1-945586-09-5

First Printing: 2018

Editing by Gwen Hoffnagle

Cover Design by Sarah Barrie of Cyanotype.ca

This publication is designed to provide accurate and authoritative information regarding the subject matter covered. It is sold with the understanding that the author is not engaged in rendering professional services. If legal, accounting, medical, psychological, or any other expert assistance is required, the services of a competent professional person should be sought. Client names have been changed to protect identities.

TABLE OF CONTENTS

INTRODUCTION

WHAT THE WORLD HEALTH ORGANIZATION SAID

In early 2018 the World Health Organization published new classifications for diseases for the upcoming International Classification of Diseases Revision 11 (ICD-11.) The ICD is a list used by medical professionals and insurance companies to categorize medical conditions. Gaming addiction is listed as a potential new disease.

The World Health Organization definition of gaming addiction:

Gaming disorder is characterized by a pattern of persistent or recurrent gaming behaviour ('digital gaming' or 'video-gaming'), which may be online (i.e., over the internet) or offline, manifested by: 1) impaired control over gaming (e.g., onset, frequency, intensity, duration, termination, context); 2) increasing priority given to gaming to the extent that gaming takes precedence over other life interests and daily activities; and 3) continuation or escalation of gaming despite the occurrence of negative consequences. The behaviour pattern is of sufficient severity to result in significant impairment in personal, family, social, educational, occupational or other important areas of functioning. The pattern of gaming behaviour may be continuous or episodic and recurrent. The gaming behaviour and other features are normally evident over a period of at least 12 months in order for a diagnosis to be assigned, although the required duration may be shortened if all diagnostic requirements are met and symptoms are severe.

(https://icd.who.int/dev11/l-m/en#/http%3A%2F%2Fid. who.int%2Ficd%2Fentity%2F1448597234)

The medical community is catching up to what parents and therapists already know. Electronic addiction is real. It can lead some young people to use electronics in ways that harm their relationships, school progress, and ability to communicate with people face to face.

In this book you'll learn about electronic addiction and practical steps you can take today to help your child use computers, gaming systems, and cell phones in a safe and balanced way. Whether your child is just starting to use electronics or spends hours online, this book provides strategies to ensure that electronics enhance your child's life instead of harm it.

SECTION 1

UNDERSTANDING ELECTRONIC ADDICTION

CHAPTER 1

THE DARK SIDE OF OUR NEW WORLD

Do any of these situations sound familiar?

Jared stays up all night playing Minecraft. There is a group of guys he plays with who are his best friends. He feels like a rock star when he creates a new world. Jared doesn't understand why his parents bug him about his homework and grades so much. School isn't important because he's going to be a video game designer or a professional YouTuber.

Tiffany desperately wants to be popular. She spends hours online researching the latest trends in makeup and fashion. When she looks at the Instagram accounts of the cool girls at her school, she knows that she isn't one of them. When a boy from math class asks her to send a photo of her naked breasts, Tiffany complies, figuring she'll have a boyfriend. And besides, he promised he wouldn't share the photo with anyone.

Matt loves his video games. He spends hours earning points, collecting weapons and potions, and killing. His ability to be stealthy and steal needed supplies helps him conquer challenges and achieve new levels in the game. He feels powerful when he beheads a dragon or an enemy. Matt got arrested for shoplifting a bag of beef jerky last week and doesn't see why it's such a big deal. He also stole his grandfather's credit card to buy Mods (extra powers) for his games.

Sarah never goes anywhere without her cell phone. It's her lifeline for keeping up with her friends, the latest gossip at school, and her celebrity crush. She loves that she can get online anytime she feels bored. When her best friend, Callie, started dating Sarah's ex-boyfriend, Sarah retaliated by posting ugly photos of Callie with the hashtag "#whore." She got her friends to forward them, so now everyone at school knows that Callie is a "total skank."

Ben spends all his free time in his room online. He comes out for meals when his mother demands it but eats quickly and goes back to his room. Ben used to have a couple of friends from the neighborhood but doesn't spend time with them anymore. He spends hours playing killing games and watching videos. Ben uses his cell phone at night to watch porn, and erases his browser history so his parents can't trace it. At seventeen, Ben has never dated or attended a school social event.

Jessica cuts herself when she feels stressed or anxious. She uses websites like icut.com, blooddrops.com, and Instagram to connect with other teens who harm themselves. Lately she's been thinking about suicide and texting about it with a girl her age she met online (at least she thinks she's her age). They are considering killing themselves on Valentine's Day.

***

I've spent the last twenty-five years working with kids and their parents in therapeutic settings. I've spoken to parents, teachers, and other counselors all over the world. Over the last ten years I've observed a disturbing trend in my psychology practice: more and more of my clients addicted to their electronic devices to the point that they are suffering significant consequences such as school failure, acts of theft, isolation, self-harm, and even suicide pacts. Others have their self-esteem destroyed by cyberbullying or get labeled as sex offenders for their online activities.

Electronic addiction is a serious issue in today's world. Most parents and educators have no idea how to spot signs of electronic addiction or help kids learn to use electronics in a healthy way. Our society unknowingly promotes electronic addiction and emphasizes only the benefits of technology. Advances in technology have provided many positive benefits; however, we are just beginning to see the addictive power of electronics and that some kids are not able to manage their use appropriately.

Today's parents are faced with challenges that did not exist when we were growing up. We had no internet, cell phones, digital cameras, or video games. We see our kids embracing technology and are amazed at how much more they know about it than we do. That makes us proud and a little sheepish. In the back of our minds we wonder if all that time online is healthy.

Electronics Are Here to Stay

In 1999 researchers started to examine the impact of electronics use on the brain, child development, and society at large. Much has been learned, but there are still many unknowns. If you are a parent of a child, you understand that it is challenging to manage electronics, and often your child knows more about how to get around parental controls than you do.

Electronics make our lives easier and more interesting. They are not going away. If you know someone in a twelve-step program for alcohol or narcotics, you know that one of the first things they learn is to avoid that substance and places where it is freely available. That's not possible with electronic addiction. Electronics are everywhere! Kids are taught to use electronics in school, homework is uploaded to the cloud, and almost every business and organization has a website to explore. Cell phones are status symbols. Can you imagine the ridicule a high school student without a cell phone would endure? Even sixth graders who don't have cell phones are taunted by peers!

Our kids are exposed to an electronic landscape that grows bigger every day. Yet few parents, schools, or religious organizations teach youths the positive and negative sides of electronics use. I've not encountered a school health class or youth organization that teaches electronic safety to the degree needed today; the technology is just too new. And the school curriculum is *way* too old!

Electronics have also changed family dynamics. When family members ride together in the car, each is plugged into an electronic device. Family conversations and game nights are forgotten activities. There are frequent arguments about not using electronics at the dinner table, and everyone in the family goes to their respective "electronic corners" after dinner.

Immediacy is our drive. We want immediate feedback and information. When we are bored, we hop on the internet or an electronic game. Parents model this behavior and even give babies cell phones to keep them quiet in the store.

I love my electronics too. While driving down the Ventura Highway to a seminar I was presenting in California, listening to the song *Ventura Highway*, it dawned on me that I had no idea where that song originated. I thought it was pretty entertaining to play *Ventura Highway* while I was traveling on the road that inspired it. So I asked Siri why they call Ventura Highway the Ventura Highway. As a person who likes to learn – not for a grade but for the sake of learning, having immediate access to knowledge is an amazing process. Google it yourself!

Those of you who are old enough to remember might recall having to go to the library and use the Dewy Decimal System to find books that provided the information you sought. Do you remember using a copy machine to collect articles for writing research papers or verbal reports, then writing notes on index cards and color-coding them? I'm thrilled that the process of locating information is so much easier today.

Premature Exposure

Honestly, I am a junky for information. I want to know why the sky and the ocean are blue. Information presents a new opportunity to discover something about the world. It is great that we can instantly find out almost anything we want to know. However, there is evidence that 60 percent of children ages twelve and above have been exposed to pornography. Even with the most vigilant parents, a child on the internet can click on something that leads them to photos of naked people and worse – even completely by accident! And older friends on the school bus show them exciting things that they have never seen before.

There are hundreds of ways that children are exposed to not just pornography, but information they are not expected to learn until they are much older. People from their elders' generations were protected from adult subjects such as violence, sexual practices, substance abuse, and even death. Exposure to these realities occurs way earlier now, desensitizing our youth to them. Some think that murder and mass shootings are normal because they hear about them and see the videos online so easily.

For example, in April of 2017 a man posted a video of himself hanging his infant daughter and then committing suicide. The website Ranker.com displays an online list of deaths from social media, providing a somewhat humorous look at murders and suicides planned and carried out online. (https://www.ranker.com/list/the-13-craziest-deaths-caused-by-social-media/whitney-milam) Imagine the damage to a young child who reads of adults and teens harming themselves and getting media attention for it. How can parents respond to this effectively?

Electronics are here to stay. We must learn how to manage them. While many kids can use electronics without problems, some are as addicted to electronics as others are to drugs or alcohol.

In *Parent's Quick Guide to Electronic Addiction* you'll learn about electronic addition and its impact on today's youth. You'll learn why electronics are so seductive and why kids, especially those who struggle with learning, mental health, or social skills, are particularly susceptible to their pull. More important you'll discover how to evaluate your child's use of electronics and take steps to curb unhealthy behaviors.

CHAPTER 2

THE NEGATIVE IMPACTS OF SOCIAL MEDIA

In April of 2017 *Harvard Business Review* published the results of an extensive study of Facebook users by Holly B. Shakya and Nicholas A. Christakis. (https://hbr.org/2017/04/a-new-more-rigorous-study-confirms-the-more-you-use-facebook-the-worse-you-feel) Prior to this study, other researchers found that the use of social media leads to poor self-esteem and depression based on users comparing their real lives to the things seen on social media. Real life can't compare to the seemingly perfect lives we believe others are enjoying online. (http://psycnet.apa.org/record/2013-25137-002)

The study by Shakya and Christakis revealed that people who used Facebook had a decrease in physical health, mental health, and satisfaction with their lives. They wrote, "While screen time, in general, can be problematic, the tricky thing about social media is that while we are using it, we get the impression that we are engaging in meaningful social interaction. Results suggest that the nature and quality of this sort of connection is no substitute for the real-world interaction we need for a healthy life."

When we use Facebook and other social media sites, we naturally compare our lives to the carefully selected photos and posts that others share. We compare our worst to their best. Some of the images and posts are not even authentic yet serve as a measuring stick that makes our lives look barren, boring, and blah.

As adults we realize that social media is often smoke and mirrors, full of advertising, fake news, and highly edited versions of life. Our kids don't have that perspective. If adults can become depressed and withdrawn after regular use of social media, just image the negative impact on kids. Young children don't know the difference between a virtual friendship and a real-life one. They can believe they are popular and have lots of friends when all they have are online strangers who might not be who they portray online.

In my practice I am working with a family who has a daughter in sixth grade. She's already had to change schools twice because she bullies others on social media. To curb the problem her parents bought her a cell phone without a camera so she could no longer spend hours posting photos online. This young lady spent an hour screaming at the top of her lungs in my office recently. She truly believes her life will be over if she cannot post on social media. Her life revolves around her electronic addiction so much that it is harming her relationships with her family members, her education, and her social development.

Facebook and other social media sites negatively impact adults' behavior as well. I've seen parents use Facebook to accuse their children's classmates of terrorism, to bully and shame other parents, and even to set up fake profiles pretending to be teens to retaliate against a former friend of their child. Shakya and Christakis found that the more time someone spends using Facebook, the more likely they are to become depressed, withdrawn, and unhealthy. Use of such social media needs to be balanced with real-world experiences!

Social media and electronics usage is a new frontier for all of us. We are just beginning to observe both the positive and negative impacts of electronics use. Our children are the first to grow up in a world based on electronics. The challenge is to understand that electronics use carries a risk for both children and adults. It has the power to seduce us and make us believe we are not as popular, attractive, skillful, or even successful at parenting as others. Too much screen time can be dangerous for adults and even more so for kids.

SocialMediaToday.com, a website for internet marketers, posted an article in January of 2017 stating that the average person spends up to two hours each day on social media sites. That usage is split between the following platforms:

- YouTube – 40 minutes
- Facebook – 35 minutes
- Snapchat – 25 minutes
- Instagram – 15 minutes
- Twitter – 1 minute

(https://www.socialmediatoday.com/marketing/how-much-time-do-people-spend-social-media-infographic)

It's even more disturbing that teens spend up to nine hours per day online, primarily via their cell phones and mobile devices. This article highlights the opportunity for businesses to market to teens via social media platforms, citing that spending on social media advertising would grow to 36 billion dollars globally in 2017.

Let those numbers sink in a moment. Spending up to nine hours per day in front of their electronics allows little time for your teen to do something more productive. When you see teens in the mall, at home, or even at school events, they have their phones in hand and are online. Many are so connected to their online world that they feel restless and uncomfortable when they cannot use their phones. Teachers must now compete with online videos and strive to hold the interest of students who are used to constant electronic stimulation.

All that sitting and looking at a computer screen takes a toll on physical health as well. In 2012 an Ohio teen was rushed to the hospital when he collapsed after playing a video game for five days straight. He was severely dehydrated. Others develop blood clots from hours of gaming. (https://www.livescience.com/22281-teens-video-games-health-risks.html) The rise in teen obesity is well documented. When I was a kid I was out camping, mowing the lawn, and playing sports with kids in the neighborhood. It never would have occurred to me to sit for eight hours in front of an electronic device. Nor would my parents ever have let me!

Advertisers realize the sales potential in marketing to teens and pour billions of dollars into influencing our children to buy or to believe they must have the latest product. Case in point: U.S. consumers spent 2.35 billion dollars on gaming in 2015. (https://www.polygon.com/2016/4/29/11539102/gaming-stats-2016-esa-essential-facts) Electronics generate big dollars, so advertisers do everything they can to attract and keep users, which includes massive marketing to our children. You've seen video games for infants and toddlers, haven't you? We are teaching our children from an early age to turn to electronics for fun, learning, and connection.

There are benefits for children who are online. They can explore the world, access new music and ideas, and even improve their eye-hand coordination and reaction time. *Science Daily* reported on the findings of a study published in the *Annals of Neurology* in 2016 that found positive benefits for children who played video games for seven hours per week or less. However, the study also found that gaming produced problems such as behavioral issues, peer conflict, and decreased social skills, especially for youths who played games for more than nine hours per week. (https://www.sciencedaily.com/releases/2016/09/160909112006.htm)

There is no precedent for the electronic age. This information is not intended to scare you. Instead, my goal is that you understand that the implications of our new electronics-based world are more far-reaching than you may realize. Video games and Facebook and other social media sites are shaping our children. Their behavior, beliefs, values, and futures are no longer the domain of parents, schools, and religious organizations, but are impacted by people who want to sell them things and by those who post things online. This is an issue of vital importance to all parents and our society at large.

The good news is that it is possible to help your child use social media and electronics wisely and in a healthy way.

CHAPTER 3

HOW DID WE GET HERE?

To understand electronic addiction, think of this simple truth: People will buy and use anything that makes life easier. It is Darwin's theory on steroids. Darwin proposed that when an organism adapts, the adaptations make it more likely to survive obstacles and reproduce. Our bodies have evolved over the millennia, making our tonsils and spleens no longer as important as they used to be. In ancient Egyptian days, people died from tooth infections. My grandfather died from a heart condition when he was younger than I am now; in today's world his heart condition would have been easily diagnosed and repaired. Our world is continually changing and adapting. Technology is an adaptation that allows us to have an easier time in life. Those who can use it will thus be the survivors of our species.

Think back and try to remember when you first discovered the internet. Remember dial-up with that crazy tone? Remember when you paid by the minute for cell phone time? Just think about how the world has adapted to internet technology in your lifetime. There are now many people who do not work in a building; they work from home. That saves money for the owner of the business, provides easier access for the business person, and saves money on commuting costs.

Did you hear about software designers, nanotechnology experts, or cybersecurity specialists when you were growing up? Those jobs did not even exist then. As our society continues to adapt to new forms of technology, more positions will be developed in technical fields. Children born today will have jobs that we can't even imagine. For example, we have already created flying cars, so could there be an air traffic controller for vehicles in the sky? Hmm... think of the possibilities of that!

Can We Blame Cell Phones?

It's hard to pinpoint the advent of electronic addiction because electronics are so interwoven in today's life. I started to see clients in my office displaying signs of electronic addiction when cell phones became affordable. Before that time most families had one shared computer, usually in a public space like the family room. Everyone in the family had to take turns using the computer, so it was easier for parents to monitor how much time was spent online.

Today's kids have laptops, gaming systems, iPods, and cell phones. It is easy for them to access the internet from any of these devices. Few parents know how to check history on a computer or cell phone. Because cell phones are handheld devices, they can be used 24/7 anywhere from a bedroom to behind the garage.

My phone is an amazing device. Once I tried to buy a phone that was just a phone, but that is almost impossible now. My phone is a phone; an answering machine; a typewriter; a dictation machine; a calendar; a weather forecaster; a stock predictor; an appointment reminder; an alarm clock (no one has an alarm clock anymore); a replacement for my home telephone (no one has a land line anymore); a remote control for my TV (yes, there is an app for that); and an entertainment device. I can watch TV, selectively blast videos, post videos of myself, and talk to my friends. It goes on and on and on.

The cell phone has become such a standard tool in our society that it has replaced other tools. No more typewriters (remember the white eraser tape?). No more telephones in the house. No more calling the weather phone number. No more calling to find out what time it is. This amazing device even does things like warn me if there is a tornado approaching, increasing my chance of survival. It alerts me if someone is armed or if there is criminal activity occurring near me – again a protection device, another adaptation for survival! It allows me to immediately contact authorities – again, a survival device.

My iPhone cost 600 bucks, which might seem like a lot, but it does so many things for me as a psychologist and lecturer that it seems worthwhile, especially since it replaces the machines I mentioned above. I can look at my calendar, respond to emails and texts, and look up new information. I can be so much more productive than I was before that the 600 bucks seems meaningless. Technology sells.

Even people who cannot afford things like clothing, food, and shelter seem to have phones. It is a status symbol. It is a survival tool. It is a computer that happens to have a telephone in it.

I could go on and on, but the point is that adaptation behooves survival; survival procreates the species; and the species evolves. So let's watch for the changes that are occurring and let's guide those changes. We should be thoughtful about how we use technology as a society. For example, giving computers to students without providing technical training or guidelines for their use can lead to disaster. Of course, there are students who can handle electronics without a problem and those who can't, but if we are going to put technology in the hands of children, we should provide ongoing training in how to use that technology appropriately.

Once I was sitting in a third-grade class that was learning about Microsoft Word. Mind you, I had used Word for many years and thought I knew how to use it effectively. The teacher told the class about a magic button. I thought she was goofing around and had no idea what she was talking about. It was the "undo" function. There had been so many times when I had made an error and wanted to reverse what I had just done, but I hadn't known about the undo button until then. Oh. My. Gosh! Dr. Berk, the university graduate and Ph.D., learned from a third-grade class that there is an undo function. It's part of mastering technology, and I was a stranger to the world these children were growing up in that was second nature to them.

The technology itself is not problematic; it is how to use and manage technology in a healthy way that we should be teaching our kids. Electronics do not kill; how people use them does.

And we should be teaching ethics alongside healthy usage. People hide behind their devices, posting things on them that they usually would not say to someone face to face. It is easy to be somebody online that you are not. It is tempting to be someone else, and being able to satisfy that temptation with no immediate repercussions can lead to the behavior becoming addictive. Lessons in ethics should be taught at home, at school, and at your place of worship. Congregations of churches, temples, and mosques should get up to date in their spiritual training to include discussions about ethics online. We didn't need to consider ethics when using typewriters, newspapers, and libraries, but we do now when opportunities to harm others instantaneously are at our fingertips. It takes a village to raise a child, and everyone in the community shares a responsibility to teach wise and ethical electronics use, beginning as soon as children are old enough to use their cell phones.

We always want the bigger, better, faster things, including electronics. Marketers know they can sell lots of electronic devices if they hit hot buttons. How many parents believe that a cell phone will keep a child safe? That's a marketing message. Parents are also told that every child needs a laptop or tablet to complete their homework. Parents who limit video-game access are often viewed as overly strict or out of date. Advertisers target kids, give them free game downloads, and then offer expensive expansion packs that make the game more fun. We are regularly being sold the idea that electronics are cool, necessary, and make life grander. They do, but they also offer kids an escape and opportunity to be someone they are not. That's where the addiction can begin.

A Gateway Drug? Sort Of.

In my practice I treat individuals with drug addiction as well as those with electronic addiction. I have observed some striking parallels in the two processes. One of my clients is a gifted young man from a good family in the suburbs. He's been off drugs for twelve months. At his last appointment he told me that he had started using heroin. When I asked him why, he said, "Dr. Berk, it feels so good. Heroin makes me feel amazing." Some of my clients who are addicted to electronics say the same thing: They feel great when they are living in the electronic world. They feel popular, skillful, smart, and connected, even when they are all alone in their bedrooms.

Because electronic addiction is a new challenge, there is not yet a formally published etiology, which is psychologist-speak for a study of its origins. Here is what I've observed about how electronic addiction develops:

- People who already have addictive personalities are particularly susceptible. Addictions often run in families. There are intergenerational patterns of addiction. Whether there is a psychological or chemical component is still being studied, but the fact remains that there are people whose personalities cause them to be more likely to become addicted, and thus the etiology exists for this to occur.

- Isolated people are more likely to be on the internet. Lack of social skills, being picked on, and being bullied push a person in this direction, which leads to a desire to escape via games or the internet.

My client who uses heroin said that alcohol initially gave him a great escape from life. Then alcohol no longer pleased him or got him high enough, so he made his way through pills, cocaine, and eventually heroin.

Understanding the etiology of an addiction includes understanding the purpose for using the addictive item – what does the gateway "drug" do for the individual? This is a vital question because all addictions meet individual needs. In electronic addiction the gateway might be computer games, which provide escape, reduce stress, and numb the brain. A kid might be clumsy and non-athletic in real life, but online he can be a football star or a powerful assassin. The game gives him a place to shine, a route to success that he can't find anywhere else. Another person might enter the addictive cycle via social media, posting photos and updates designed to make them feel popular and part of the in-crowd at school. The attention they get online replaces the social isolation they are experiencing in their daily life. Treatment and intervention start with uncovering the underlying need.

The problem is that as with any high, you are always chasing the same high, and to do so you must increase your use or increase the amount of the drug. Electronic games are wired to get to the next level, get the next kill, get the next object, etc., and we are wired to follow through with that. They also provide an escape in times of pain, stress, or anxiety, helping users avoid things they do not want to do or feel.

The following are just some of the "gateways" that make kids more likely candidates for electronic addiction:

- Bullying
- Over-emphasis on fitting in
- Previous mental health or behavioral issues
- Low self-esteem
- Self-harm
- Social isolation or feeling that no one else has similar interests
- Learning problems that make them feel incompetent
- Depression, anxiety, or other mental health challenges
- Family challenges that create a desire to escape
- A general lack of success with traditional tasks of adolescence such as school, extracurricular activities, friendships, social engagement, dating, and employment

CHAPTER 4

SIGNS OF AN ELECTRONIC ADDICTION

One of my favorite professors at Cleveland State University taught me that addiction is when your behavior starts having a negative impact and you keep using despite negative consequences. I think this is also the best description of electronic addiction. Although there are various inventories and assessments available to determine whether someone is addicted to electronics, if your child overuses them despite negative consequences you should get involved whether or not your child agrees it's an issue.

When I see someone in my office I look for these issues as a sign of a potential electronic addiction:

- **Isolation:** The child no longer has friends they interface with daily or with whom they have a deep relationship. They would rather seek out electronic friends who share the same interests than kids from school or the neighborhood. In this situation the child is missing out on social-skills development such as how to share, compromise, tease without hurting, etc. Many of these kids already have deficits in social skills and their electronic isolation does not give them opportunities to improve.

Watch out for *parallel play*, which is when kids are playing video games side by side while not talking to each other or interacting with each other. They are together, but there are fewer interactions than when kids engage in non-electronic activities.

- **Irritability:** When a child overreacts to losing at games, is irritable due to loss of sleep, or responds inappropriately to a parent's request to stop using electronics, it is a definite sign that the child is starting to have an addiction issue. Irritability is compounded by sleep issues and things they find frustrating. Just as a gambler can move from compulsion to addiction, irritability is a sign that an obsession or compulsion is becoming a more significant issue.

My aunt, who is a lovely person, worked as a saleslady her entire life. When she retired she took trips to Atlantic City and Las Vegas to try gambling. She became enthralled with Vegas, and over time lost everything she had. Once she asked me to pay her rent. I offered to send the money directly to the landlord so she would have a place to live and would not gamble the money. She became very irritable and would not talk to me anymore. This is an extreme measure of irritability, but an example of what can happen when things don't go the person's way.

I know kids who punch holes in the walls of their home when parents take away their game controllers or cell phones. Or they simply steal them back! One young man destroyed his mother's precious tea set, inherited from her grandmother, when he was forbidden online access. Others become very upset when they can't beat a level in a game or if the internet goes down. Irritability with self and others is a particularly strong indicator of an electronic addiction, especially when coupled with physical or verbal aggression.

- **Money-seeking:** Stealing or borrowing money you cannot repay is a typical sign of an addicted gambler. What I have seen with addicted gamers is that they use their parents' credit cards without permission to purchase expansion packs or other gaming enhancements. The parents won't turn them in to the police because they do not want them to have a criminal record. Some kids borrow money from peers and then steal money from their parents to pay off the debt. I know of a young lady who pawned her mother's and grandmother's wedding rings to feed her electronic addiction.

- **Relationship changes:** Most children change their relationships with their immediate family members when they become adolescents. Withdrawing to their rooms and spending more time with their friends than with family are typical adolescent changes. However, when they isolate themselves in their rooms and spend no time with friends, that is a signal to be concerned. They might be losing friends because they are addicted to their electronic devices.

- **Accessing adult websites:** Both boys and girls are getting more and more access to pornography online. Even though pornography has always been around, today it is much easier to access, it is much more explicit, and it can certainly make an impact, especially on young children. I worked with a young teen who was addicted to watching videos depicting anal sex and people inserting objects into their rectums. He becomes stimulated by these videos and masturbates. This is a serious concern for safety reasons and because of the potential for negatively impacting his behavior as an adult.

- **No desire to try typical peer activities:** Addicted kids often drop out of activities such as marching band, sports, scouting, and other common youth activities, which isolates them and puts them in a position in which their sole connection is online.

- **Loss of close friends:** Loss of close friends, also called "friend-friends," – real-world friends who invite them to sleepovers, to sit together at lunch, or to go bowling or to a sporting event – is a sign that something is not right in their life. (You'll learn more about this in chapter 10.)

- **Aggression:** Some children I work with become very aggressive as a result of losing their gaming privileges. They often become verbally aggressive, and even on some occasions become physically aggressive. They use the retaliatory theory: if you take their games, they will take your things to get back at you.

- **Others point out their addiction:** Be interested enough in your child's acquaintances to pick up on it if someone expresses concern. You can ask your child, "Have your friends or anyone else brought up your overuse of electronics?" The most common answer is, "All my friends do the same thing I do." That can be the case, but often it is because they are narrowing down their field of friends to those who are similar to them and do the same things.

- **Poor choice of peer groups:** It's normal for kids to change friends and peer groups as they age. Responsibly done, this is not a bad thing; however, when done in an unhealthy way it can become a problem. If your child has started hanging out with peers who demonstrate negative behaviors, they can be exposed to information they are not ready to process. They can also be manipulated into situations that feel overwhelming. A shift to a different peer group is not a negative thing in itself, but it should come about without coercion or harm to anyone.

- **Lack of balance:** There should be a balance between how much time your child spends online and how much time they spend doing other things. If you observe your child's world shrinking to the point that they find fun or satisfaction only when gaming or online, there is a problem to address.

CHAPTER 5

WAYS ELECTRONIC ADDICTION MANIFESTS

Gender-Specific Triggers

In my practice I see more males with electronic addiction than females. While it occurs in both genders, it is caused by different needs and manifests in different ways in males than it does in females.

Males are usually addicted to things that produce an adrenalin hit such as video games and pornography. Adolescent males experience many sexual impulses and get erections easily. Pornography provides an immediate release of sexual tension, especially for someone who is too shy to talk to a live girl. Most games are designed to trigger a dopamine release in the brain every three to five seconds, which is very rewarding for the male brain. And reaching goals in video games creates a sensation of competence and dominance. Males enjoy conquering obstacles, reaching new levels, and learning tricks to increase their performance. Gaming provides an environment of challenge and the ability to conquer. Boys even enjoy watching others play video games so that they can learn new tricks.

Males can base their self-esteem on their gaming performance. They like to compare the levels they reached or their number of kills to those of others. Video games in which you kill characters were developed by the military to train soldiers and entailed a lot of internal stress and pressure to perform well. Some boys get so frustrated when they fail in a game that they throw their controls against the wall, or "rage quit. *Rage-quitting* is also a term used by gamers for people who quit in the middle of a group game when they are losing. Explosive outbursts while video gaming can be a signal that your child is taking their gaming too seriously.

Electronic addiction in females usually looks very different. Adolescent girls want to be admired and garner social acceptance. They want to be seen, followed, and envied. They focus on social media, looking at what others are doing on Snapchat, Instagram, and Facebook so they can feel like they are in the popular crowd. Many spend hours watching to see what others post about them. Some obsessively watch YouTube videos about makeup, fashion, or how to attract a boyfriend. Some enjoy making videos and collecting attention for their desirability, knowledge, or coolness. Adolescent girls can be very mean and bully others on social media, believing that excluding someone means they themselves will be included or admired.

Fear of Missing Out

F.O.M.O. is a popular acronym that stands for fear of missing out, which is a contributing factor to electronic addiction in many people. Socially anxious, depressed, isolated kids, and those on the autism spectrum, are particularly vulnerable to FOMO. When people see posts online of others attending parties, having fun with friends, dating, or engaging in exciting activities, they fear that their lives are boring and that they are missing all the fun that others are having. They are desperate to fit in and be included in groups they perceive as popular or cool. Being excluded can be terribly upsetting to them.

FOMO can lead to creating a false online personality who has a boyfriend or girlfriend, has no rules at home, or has tried drugs or alcohol, in an attempt to get others to envy them. Some use photo-editing software to create fake photos that support their online persona.

FOMO can also lead to bullying. Kids can believe that if they exclude unpopular kids they will be accepted by those seen as popular. The drive to be accepted and part of a popular group can be a strong motivator for kids, contributing to electronic addiction and maladaptive behavior. It is important for parents to educate their kids about the hazards of false postings and photos. Young people often don't realize that just because something is on the internet doesn't make it true.

Types of Electronic Addictions

Children become addicted to electronics based on past experiences, environment, and psychosocial factors. Following is a general overview of the kinds of electronic addictions I have observed in my work with kids:

- **Gamers:** It's common for gamers to become addicted because they seek the exhilaration of reinforcement that comes every few seconds in a video game. Their identity becomes who they are online. Their online personality becomes more important than their real-life personality, so they want to stay in the electronic world. Many games base the self-esteem of the player on their ability to win, conquer levels, or feel powerful in a fantasy world.

- **Loners:** Kids who are outsiders often would rather be a part of a group. Many of the loners I meet in my practice are also transgender, gay, or have unusual interests, and seek others who are like them. For example, if you have an interest in squids you can find an online squid group and feel like less of a loner. This connection helps you feel accepted and comfortable, so it can develop into an addiction. It can also make it very difficult to relate to people at school and in the community who don't share the squid connection.

- **Explorers:** It's great when kids love to expand their knowledge, but if they spend all their time doing so online and don't complete their homework or participate in other activities, it has become a problem. This type of electronic addiction occurs most frequently in those on the autism spectrum.

- **Escapers:** Kids in this group want to escape into the world of electronics because real life is too painful. They love fantasy and often create personas that are more powerful or successful than they feel in their daily lives. Most of these individuals have experienced trauma such as abandonment, bullying, learning problems, loss of friendship, isolation, or rejection. Many in this group have a comorbid diagnosis, meaning they suffer from more than one medical condition. (You'll learn more about the combination of a mental health challenge and an electronic addiction in chapter 6.)

- **Kids with anger issues:** Unfortunately, we see hate-mongering on the internet nowadays – from those who persecute others and even from terrorist groups. Many adolescents have anger issues, and viewing this material is dangerous to them. When they get online and find material that stokes their anger, their subsequent behavior can have serious consequences.

- **Kids with poor social skills:** For those who are shy, socially awkward, anxious, or rejected by their peers, the electronic world can provide a haven for acceptance. This can be a positive experience; however, these children are often targets for predators and those seeking a naive person to manipulate. It is vital to determine whether your child is using the electronic world to hide away from the real world or can balance online time with time spent with others.

Do your homework. Find out what other adults have to say about your child. Do teachers observe that your child interacts with friends, or are they sitting alone at lunch every day? It can be challenging to get this information, especially regarding middle school and high school students whose teachers often do not observe them outside of the classroom. Some students don't even go to the lunchroom and just wander the halls or hang out where teachers don't see them.

Ask the school counselor if they would be willing to observe your child outside the classroom and report back to you. The lunch period allows for unstructured social interaction, so problems with peers might surface during that time. The counselor might balk at this request, especially if your child does not exhibit behavior problems. If your child is quiet, they are probably ignored even though quiet kids such as the loners and escapers described above can be facing social challenges. Be assertive and continue to work with the school counselor to get the information you need.

Take proactive steps to determine if your child has an electronic addiction. There are many practical ideas waiting for you in section 2.

CHAPTER 6

MENTAL HEALTH ISSUES AND THE COLLISION WITH ELECTRONIC ADDICTION

It is almost impossible to separate mental health issues from electronic addiction; there is a strong link between them. It is the proverbial chicken and egg situation in that it is difficult to know which came first. If your child has one of the following mental health challenges, they might be prone to use electronics as a coping mechanism.

- **Depression:** Many people with depression escape into the online world. It offers seemingly accepting people, many of whom have similar challenges. These people become your child's close friends and confidants. Depression leads to isolation, which leads to interacting with others online who also feel rejected and isolated. The remedy is to have the child get therapy and get involved with peers with whom they can connect in person. A psychologist who has a breadth of experience can sort out the underlying reasons for the depression, and it's vital that the depression itself be addressed by a professional. Therapy addresses the reasons the client is drawn to the online world. Treat the cause. When electronic addiction is a manifestation of depression, getting to the root cause of the depression is paramount to a successful outcome. Your child could be struggling with an undiscovered learning disability or processing problem, poor social skills, or other developmental challenges that are causing frustration, isolation, and depression.

- **Learning disorder:** Academic challenges including processing issues, dyslexia, and other learning disorders often lead to failure at school. The frustration builds, and the child looks for an escape. Academic challenges lead to feelings of shame, incompetence, and isolation, which lead to finding friends online instead of in the real world. Kids with learning disorders are not very good at schoolwork but they can be skilled at gaming and finding internet chat rooms. It is essential to get to the underlying symptomatology, which requires academic and developmental testing and assessment to understand the learning issue. If you suspect a learning challenge, ask your school district personnel to provide testing. Some district administrators do not test children simply because they are asked to, so you might have to engage a psychologist or learning specialist yourself. The longer a child struggles with a learning disability the more difficult it is to make up for lost time at school, so do this sooner rather than later.

- **Self-injurious behavior:** Unfortunately, self-injury has become the hot rage, especially for teenaged girls. Fueled mostly by the internet, self-injury does have its purpose – it works to some degree yet can cause dangerous health risks and deep scarring. One must look at the underlying causes of self-injury, which can be attention-seeking, release of emotions, or social connectedness. Work with your child's therapist to determine the underlying causes. Once those are identified, try these interventions:

o **For attention-seeking:** If your child is cutting for attention, help them do something that makes them feel good. Focus on what they do well. Try to get them involved in volunteering or helping others. Kids who cut themselves where others will notice it are generally seeking attention. They require therapeutic help to uncover why they need more attention and to find positive ways to generate it.

o **For emotional release:** This is the most addictive form of self-harm. The child cuts where it cannot be seen, such as their armpits, upper arms, inner thighs, or crotch. They often wear long sleeves even on hot days to hide the cuts. They feel an emotional release when they harm themselves. Along with therapy they need sunshine, healthy endorphins from exercise, and other positive experiences.

o **For social connection:** The cutting culture is very accepting. All that is needed for instant acceptance is to harm yourself. There are many websites devoted to self-harm and how to do it easily. Kids who harm themselves to create social connections need to bond with a new, positive peer group immediately. See if you can get an adult to invite them to join a group. It's best if a friend is invited along with them or is already in the group. Consider school clubs, religious organizations, community theatre, and other groups where they can feel a sense of belonging. These kids also require support from a therapist.

- **ADHD:** Attention deficit hyperactivity disorder causes kids to be always on the move. They get bored easily and seek constant stimulation. The stimulation can be online where they surf the net, play games, and move from video to video to combat boredom. They tend to use other stimulants while they are online, such as energy drinks that keep them "hyped." The best solution for kids with ADHD is to stay active. They need an alternative high. Consider BMX racing, skateboarding, swimming, diving, rock climbing, and other physical activities that provide a rush of adrenaline. If your child is not athletic, performing in community theatre, a musical group, a community volunteer effort, or another complex or stimulating activity can provide an exciting challenge. If not engaged in such an activity, the lure of gaming can become a problem.

- **Personality disorder:** This is a controversial area, as some believe that personality disorders cannot be diagnosed in young people. However, some children face personality challenges early in life. I believe these are genuine personality disorders, and some of them draw adolescents to addictive behavior. For example, kids with budding personality disorders love to stir things up, and social media is a great place to do that. Posting pictures of a group doing something fun without a targeted individual, and posting unflattering photos of a particular person, are great ways to create drama. Teach your child to block people who like to bully or cause friction on social media. If your child is the one stirring things up, social media is particularly dangerous for them. It is too easy to bully, exclude others, and retaliate on social media against real or perceived slights from others. Work closely with a therapist to determine the best approach to social media use if you suspect your child is developing a personality disorder.

- **Conduct disorder:** Adolescents with conduct disorder often become adults with antisocial personality disorder – not someone you want to meet in a dark alley. I have clients with conduct disorder who are hooked on games. They are often also hooked on pornography and other ways to get high. One of my clients is addicted to pornography and also seeks stimulation through inhaling felt-tipped markers. Even though he knows that "huffing" is dangerous to his health, he continues to do it. He also steals – a thrill-seeking behavior. Although he is a very nice young man in many ways, he lacks an empathy chip. Electronics offer him the opportunity to reach out to a world he is not ready to handle. We are limiting his electronic exposure and steering him into a vocational program so he can use his hands more and feel successful.

- **Oppositional defiant disorder:** Someone with this disorder thrives on defying authority. They argue frequently, see other people as the cause of problems, and do whatever they are told *not* to do. This disorder sometimes occurs alongside depression, anxiety, and/or autism. Kids with this challenge are masters at finding exceptions to every rule, and have fun proving others wrong. They are very susceptible to stealing money and credit cards to fund their electronic addiction and to venturing into the dark web.

If your child has oppositional defiant disorder, they need control. It is very important to prearrange consequences of their actions to reduce the potential for arguments. Use a format like this: "If you don't follow the rule about no electronics after nine p.m., you'll lose your phone for twenty-four hours." Be sure they turn in their phone and electronic devices to you at bedtime so they will not be tempted to lie and say they were not on the phone at 3:00am, even if they were.

- **Anxiety disorder:** Wow! If you are anxious, hit the internet and it will make you even more anxious. Information can be scary. Anxious people often seek information on the internet about ways to calm themselves or numb their feelings, and it can be a useful tool if they watch relaxation or mindfulness videos. We don't want to throw out the baby with the bathwater regarding what should and should not be accessed online, but for people with anxiety disorder, the best treatment we have is *cognitive behavioral therapy*, which can also help with comorbid conditions and reduce the need to escape via the internet.

Individuals with electronic addiction almost always struggle with anxiety, especially regarding social situations. They have challenges making eye contact, participating in small talk, and finding others who enjoy the same things they enjoy. Kids who are homeschooled and struggle with anxiety are particularly challenged because their opportunities for social interaction with peers are very limited. If you are homeschooling your child, pay close attention to their electronics use, provide extra opportunities to interact with others offline, and educate them thoroughly about safety online.

My son suffers from seasickness. We recently went on a harbor cruise in a very calm harbor, and he became seasick just anticipating how he would feel if the waters became choppy. In the same way, people with anxiety often anticipate having a problem in the future, which causes as much anxiety as something more tangible. They might worry about talking with others in the lunch room and wander the halls during lunch instead of eating. Anticipatory anxiety can result in electronic addiction because you can avoid interacting directly with others when interacting with them from the safety of your electronic device.

- **Autism and the internet – a perfect storm:** Satoshi Tajiri loved insects. As a young lad with Asperger syndrome, he spent hours in his native Japan studying bugs. Other kids teased him and called him Dr. Bug. His parents were worried about his poor grades and habit of cutting classes to play games at the local arcade. When video games were developed he became obsessed with finding out how they worked. Tajiri went on to create Pokémon, one of the most successful games ever created.

Tajiri's story highlights the positive influence that electronics can have for kids with autism spectrum disorders. But kids with autism are also perfectly poised to be hit by electronic addiction. Many people with electronic addiction have trouble reading interpersonal cues such as eye contact, facial expressions, and body language. None of that is required on the internet. For example, many people with autism spectrum challenges look at people's eyebrows instead of their facial expressions.

Kids with autism can be very rigid about their routines. They struggle with transitions – from simple changes in their daily schedule to major changes such as moving to a new home. This rigidity can lead to constant battles at home, so some parents are reluctant to argue with them about computer use. They can develop a distinctive interest like dinosaurs or trains and not want to do anything that is not related to that interest.

I often joke with my clients. In one group I said to a boy with ADHD, "If you don't sit still I am going to rip your arm off and beat you with the bloody, stumpy end of your arm." He laughed, but the child with autism said, "Dr. Berk, you can't do that. That would be child abuse." That is an example of the black-and-white thinking so prevalent in people with autism spectrum disorders. Because these kids struggle with reading social cues and facial expressions, the online world is more comfortable to navigate because it's black and white. For example, ALL-CAPS ARE USED IF SOMEONE IS YELLING, and lowercase if they're not. It's a very simple code; much less subtle than a smirk versus a smile.

Here's an example from my therapy practice: A child asked me, "Dr. Berk, if I'm walking to the lunch room and someone is waving to me, inviting me to his lunch table, and smiling, how do I know if I should go there or not?" I asked him, "Is it a friend of yours?" He answered, "Well, he is what you would call an acquaintance friend, Dr. Berk." I asked, "Is he smiling or smirking?" The child looked at me perplexed. "What do you mean a smile or a smirk?" I said, "A smile is a big smile, a smirk is kind of halfway." He was puzzled and replied, "If I go to the table and he's really a friend, he's going to let me sit there. If I go to the table and he's not, he's going to dump milk on me or make fun of me, and I don't want to be made fun of." I encouraged this young man to bring up this topic in his social-skills group. One of his peers gave this wise advice: "Walk towards the table. Keep walking and watch him. Does he look at you and keep smiling, or does he look at his friends and then look at you and look at his friends and look at you? If he is doing that, walk away. If he is looking at you the whole time, go and sit with him."

Many people with autism have sensory challenges. They do not like being around other people who make noises or bother them. Sensory challenges include crowds, noises, certain foods, and even certain clothing. For example, people on the autism spectrum usually don't wear jeans because they're stiff. They don't like tight-fitting clothes, scratchy clothes, or tags in their clothing. A child who is on the autism spectrum experiences so much discomfort in the real world that they are very prone to escaping into the perceived safety of the electronic world. When you're on the internet you can wear anything you want to and nobody judges you. If your child seems to have sensory challenges, request a consultation with an occupational therapist, as many sensory challenges can be reduced through treatment.

Kids with autism disorders can also be easily fooled and manipulated. With their black-and-white thinking, they can be tricked into believing a scam or trusting someone who wants to harm them. They need help determining what is real and what is not real, especially online.

- **Addiction:** Addictions run in families, and I believe electronic addiction runs in families as well. People in my age group were seldom exposed to machines that could become addictive. There were only three channels on TV, hardly enough to support addictive behavior. It is different now. Today's parents often struggle with their own addictions. They might have a drug, alcohol, or shopping addiction – same prize, different package, so to speak. If there is addictive behavior in your family, warn your child that they are likely to be pulled towards addiction as well, and help them recognize the signs.

The Yum Factor

I mentioned my favorite professor in an earlier chapter. I'll never forget the day he talked about the "yum factor." He taught us that some bodies have a yum factor. This means that when they are exposed to an addictive substance like drugs, alcohol, or pornography, they respond with "YUM." The yum factor is part of any kind of addiction, including electronic addiction. It has to do with serotonin levels and neurotransmitters, and kicks in strongly in certain children when they are exposed to electronics.

Remember Pong, one of the first electronic games? Pong consisted of a dot that went back and forth across the computer screen like a ping pong ball on a ping pong table. Players maneuvered a "paddle" to hit the ball, and the paddle got smaller as the ball went faster. That was it. Today we have first-person shooter games such as Assassins Creed and Call of Duty. When a player gets a kill, they get rewarded with better weapons, points, or powers, which makes them feel powerful and successful. These games elicit the yum factor. It's where kids with the yum factor get their identity. "I have so many kills," they say. "I am the greatest at [whatever game it is]." I might ask them, "How long did it take you to get to that level?" "Well, I played for forty-eight hours straight." "Forty-eight hours straight?" "Yeah. I slept a little bit, but I played the whole weekend."

Today's video games appeal to a different part of the brain than the ones that were being developed when I was young. They seek to make you something you are not: "I may not be anything at school, but I am the greatest sniper on the planet." The fantasy draws you in. The yum factor is very understandable, especially for children who inherit a tendency towards addiction from their relatives, and for those who want to escape reality.

As you can see, there is a clear link between mental health challenges and a propensity for electronic addiction. It makes sense that an isolated kid who feels unsuccessful in school, unattractive, or socially awkward would find the online world alluring. It's all too easy for them to drift into a situation in which all their friendships, entertainment, and pleasure come from the online world. If your child has a mental health challenge, be extra vigilant about electronic addiction.

CHAPTER 7

ELECTRONIC ADDICTION AND CHILD DEVELOPMENT

In my practice I see kids with a variety of challenges during their formative years. Recently I've noticed a disturbing trend: kids who are online a lot make less eye contact and display poor conversational skills. They are used to being in the electronic world, so when they are forced to wait or to participate in a conversation that is not interesting to them, they turn to their phones for entertainment. When phone use is not permitted, they can become very frustrated and uncomfortable. Many of these kids have difficulty with negotiation, coping with authority, knowing when to stop arguing and concede a point, and giving and receiving feedback. They are intelligent, but lack mastery of tasks that require face-to-face conversation with a variety of people.

Many of these kids also lack a clear understanding of the value we place on privacy. They can be shocked by an angry reaction to their posting a video of a sibling or classmate. Some use social media to air their grievances with a teacher, friend, romantic partner, or parent, never considering that their actions are inappropriate or an invasion of another's privacy.

Erik Erickson was a developmental psychologist who created a theory of psychosocial development based on how people socialize and develop their sense of self. Erickson's theory posits that each stage of life presents certain psychosocial tasks to be mastered. These tasks serve as building blocks. As each stage is mastered, it leads to the next one. Erickson believed that all people go through these developmental stages in the same order, but the timeline can vary based on personal limitations or experiences. Parents should have a basic understanding of these developmental stages so they can monitor their child's progress through them.

Erickson's Developmental Stages:

1. **Trust versus mistrust – infancy to eighteen months:** Babies enter an uncertain world. They are dependent on their parents for everything including food, shelter, and protection. When they receive care, they develop hope and learn to trust that others will help them in times of crisis.

2. **Autonomy versus shame and doubt – ages eighteen months to three years:** Toddlers become more independent as they learn to do things for themselves such as selecting toys, feeding themselves, and dressing. They learn that they have a will and can make decisions on their own, not depending on their parents for everything.

3. **Initiative versus guilt – ages three to five:** Young children learn by playing alone and with others. In this stage they learn to have a purpose by asking questions, exploring their world through their senses, and initiating interactions with others.

4. **Industry versus inferiority – ages five to twelve:** In this stage children enter school and their peer group becomes very important. They learn to master skills like reading and writing and athletics, and to complete chores at home. This mastery helps them feel competent and develop healthy self-esteem. They learn how to fail and recover, realizing that they cannot do everything well but that all people have strengths and challenges. When a child in this stage has a learning or developmental disorder, they might start to feel that they are inferior to their peers. Electronic addiction can begin in this developmental stage. They are exposed to electronics at school, observe peers enjoying them, and might fear missing out on the fun they believe others are experiencing.

5. **Identity versus role confusion – ages twelve to eighteen:** This stage of life is full of challenges. Adolescents explore various roles, who they are, and what paths they would like to take in the future. Peers become more important than parents and other adults. It is a confusing time of physical, mental, emotional, and social change. It is a time of experimentation, rebellion, and growth as they discover their own identity. Adolescents develop self-control and self-regulation as they learn to manage their time and emotions. Electronic addiction can become a serious problem in this stage, leading to isolation and a distorted view of self and the world.

6. **Intimacy versus isolation – ages eighteen to forty:** In young adulthood people learn to trust others and share themselves with others in professional and

romantic situations. They enter the workforce, date with an eye to a long-term relationship, and explore long-term relationships. If they didn't experience close real-world friendships before this stage, they can struggle with intimacy from both a lack of understanding what intimacy is and from a lack of relationship skills. They need to develop an understanding of themselves to share their lives with another. If they have been relating to others only in the online world where they can live through a contrived persona, they will struggle to create honest and meaningful relationships. People who do not successfully embrace their true identity and connect with others based on that identity can suffer from isolation and depression.

(https://www.simplypsychology.org/Erik-Erikson.html)

(There are two other developmental stages in Erickson's theory, but they are not germane to our discussion in this book.)

As you can see, each stage of child development requires a deepening ability to interact with the world and other people. Effective communication becomes more and more critical. We learn by participating in life, failing, succeeding, and trying again, while interactions with family members, teachers, peers, community members, and authority figures provide opportunities for learning and development. I believe that being isolated by electronic devices impacts these stages. *Electronic isolationism* is a term I use to describe individuals who lack enough contact with the real world to foster healthy social and emotional growth.

Loss of Empathy

In 2012 Berkley professor Ronald Dahl published a research review on adolescent development that included studies about empathy. This research found that at certain times the teenaged brain was unable to successfully recognize and respond to others' emotions. While you might not be familiar with this study, if you have a teen in your home you might be familiar with the evidence: Your sweet child seems to disappear, replaced by an angry, moody person who doesn't seem to care about anyone.

This time of emotional turmoil starts to ebb for girls around age thirteen as they begin to recognize the impact of their words and actions on others. Boys, however, experience a decline in empathy from ages thirteen to sixteen. According to this study, the brains of boys in that age range cannot process others' emotions successfully. This processing problem might be linked to rising levels of testosterone and to societal pressures to act like a man by being tough, strong, and humorous. Thankfully a boy's ability to empathize returns around age sixteen and they can catch up to their female peers. (https://www.ncbi.nlm.nih.gov/pubmed/22903221)

Lack of Real-World Skills

Now that you have a bit of background on child development, you can see that every challenge and interaction during the childhood and adolescent years has a purpose. Each experience serves to help kids grow in skills, self-understanding, and the ability to relate to others and the world. When kids spend hours online they miss out on many of those opportunities.

When I was young, my friends and I created games. And we refereed our games. We included everybody. We learned social skills in the neighborhood and on the playground. We argued over who was out and who was safe during baseball games. We called for do-overs if we could not find a solution. Those experiences taught us to debate, win and lose gracefully, and maintain friends during times of disagreement. Our children are not learning those skills in front of their computer screens.

For many years I led youth backpacking and canoeing trips to Canada, spending ten days on an island with a bunch of kids. They had to learn to get along with each other, pitch tents, make fires, cook meals, and navigate the wilderness. What I found interesting was that they did not know what to do with free time. I noticed very quickly that if we were canoeing, pumping water, making fires, or preparing meals, there were few problems. The problems came during free time. They would look at me and say, "What are we supposed to do?" I suggested things like devising a swimming competition, making rafts, building treehouses, or playing hide and seek in the woods. They looked at me as if I were crazy, and had no idea how to organize or run games themselves. I realized I had to fill the time for them and created activities like the "Burly Bear Olympics" and other competitions.

Think wisely about this. It is unfair to blame our children for this because they are coming into a world in which they do not get exposed to many opportunities to fill their own time without electronics. Because many kids have fewer neighborhood friends than we did when I was young, they don't have as many opportunities to try new things. It is incumbent on parents to expose them to activities they have not tried such as fishing, scuba diving, camping, art, and music. Activities done as a family can provide fun, bonding, and an opportunity for parents to model the joy of trying something new. (You'll find suggestions for this in chapter 9.)

Let me share with you one of my favorite moments. Picture two sixteen-year-old boys wearing life jackets, arguing in a canoe in the middle of a lake. The boat is filled with backpacks, water bottles, and fishing gear. They continue arguing and then they stand up. One would think that they would realize it's not wise to stand up in a canoe, but no. I was sitting in a canoe very near them, supervising them and making sure all was safe, watching the scene unfold like a movie. I said to them, "You might want to resolve this issue sitting down, because it's a wet lake there and if you fall in and get your gear wet, there is nowhere to dry it out." But they continued to argue and each threw a punch at the other. Of course, they flipped the canoe in the middle of the lake. No one was hurt, but the point is that these kids had never been in a canoe before, did not have any boating skills, and could not control their emotions enough to predict the outcome of their actions.

Spending hours in front of a screen removes from today's kids the opportunities we had to learn about the world and other people. Recreation now consists of playing games online with people all over the world. My clients say, "I'm playing with my friends." "Are these really your friends?" I ask. "Of course they're my friends. I meet with them every night. We play. We talk. They are my great friends."

An Easier Path to the Tasks of Adolescence

Children go through many changes in the years from infancy to adulthood. The adolescent years are particularly challenging. Remember the terror of standing against the wall at the school dance, arguments with your parents, riding the bench instead of being a starter, painful breakups, and all the mistakes you made in your teens? Those years were hard for us, and they are even more challenging for our kids.

It's easy to understand why many teens are drawn to the electronic world where they can be whoever they want to be without struggle. They can create an online persona who is smarter or more attractive, athletic, or popular than they feel in real life. If they want sex, they can skip dating and look at online porn or go to Tinder and find a hookup. If they want to feel powerful, they can conquer worlds or kill hundreds of bad guys in their video games. If they are tired of studying, they can buy research papers or copies of exams and improve their grades. If they feel alone, they can quickly connect with others who share their interests in medieval swords, fashion, or heavy metal music. When they are bored, they can numb-out by watching hours of videos on YouTube or bingeing on Netflix.

In some ways all these online activities can be seen as a smart adaptation to life. The electronic world provides a faster, easier path to the tasks of adolescent development. Kids can't see the danger in it or the missed opportunities to develop relationships and experiences that will shape their adult lives. It is our responsibility as parents to help them use electronics wisely and balance their lives with real experiences. It's not easy, as this is new territory for us, too; however, it's possible, and it's worth the effort to invest in the healthy future of your child.

The process starts with awareness of the developmental stages and the impact of too much time spent on electronics. As you continue to read this book you'll learn specific techniques for helping your child learn to use electronics in a healthy and balanced way that supports their social and personal development.

SECTION 2

WHAT PARENTS CAN DO ABOUT ELECTRONIC ADDICTION

CHAPTER 8

CREATING A BALANCED ELECTRONIC LANDSCAPE

There are many things you can do to help prevent or reduce the impact of electronic addiction for your child, but doing nothing is a bad plan. It may be that your child will just grow out of electronic addiction like other childhood phases, but there is a strong possibility that they will not. Consider acting to hedge that possibility.

Action earlier is better than action later. The longer someone engages in addictive behavior, the harder it is to break. Early intervention is the key to recovery from electronic addiction, as it is with addictions to alcohol, drugs, and gambling. Prevention and intervention should start early.

When your child is young, showering them with electronic toys and gifts begins the process. I will never forget what my Uncle Al told me when I became a parent: "Watch when your son is little. When people bring toys over, your son will probably want to play with the box more than the toy." Uncle Al was right. He also told me that his favorite toy was a wooden spoon. I remember the best gift I ever received as a kid was the refrigerator box. I was out in the yard playing with the box for hours and days, until it rained and the box fell apart.

Begin setting limits on electronics when your child is an infant. If you overuse them with your baby, you are setting them up for a lifetime of dependency. As they get older, balance electronic gifts with ones that foster imagination. Don't be afraid to say no if they too often reach for the electronic toy; moderation is the key. When my children were young, electronic toys were just coming out. Their favorite uncle bought them each Xboxes. We graciously returned them and said that we would rather have non-electronic gifts. If your child receives a gift that makes you uncomfortable, you have a right to return it.

Don't overlook that your child will do what mine did and play video games at other people's houses. You probably cannot limit that as much as you think you can, but try. The funniest thing I overheard was when my son was riding in the backseat with his friend, and the friend asked him about video games, and my son said, "We don't have electronics at the house." My son's friend was shocked and asked, "You don't have electricity at your house?"

It is important to have clear rules for your child about using electronics when visiting others. Teach your child what to do if they are teased because they can't play games that others do. You can even encourage your child to blame you and say something like "My mom will kill me if she catches me playing that game." If that doesn't solve the problem, encourage your child to tell you when they have been invited to play video games or surf the web so that you can call the other parent and share your family rules for electronics.

An Electronic Landscape

It is important to decide when your child can and cannot use electronics and to establish those rules for them, taking their age and developmental stage into consideration. Have a family discussion so your child understands the reasoning behind the rules. I call this an "electronic landscape" – a healthy set of guidelines that govern electronics use in your home.

Create flexible rules that accommodate the seasons. If you live in a place where it is snowy and rainy in the winter, you can allow more screen time then than on bright summer days. Consider rules for electronics use during the school week and other options for weekends and vacations. If you create this plan with your child, they will not feel quite as put-upon, but prepare for complaints. It's up to you to set the standards and make the tough calls, even if you get some flak from your child. You ensure that they brush their teeth and go to the dentist even when they don't like it, and the same goes for electronics. Limiting electronics use is not going to be a popular decision, but it is important for their health.

Learn about video games and what they contain. The ratings are there for a reason, whether it be violence, sexual content, or strong language. Ask the clerk at the store for advice. Consider your child's maturity level as well has their chronological age. Some older kids can handle sexual content, but regardless of their age they should not be exposed to more violence than what is already unavoidable in the media. You know your child best, so follow your instincts regarding what types of games you allow them to play.

The earlier you can create this electronic landscape, the easier honoring it will be for both you and your child. If you are just learning about electronic addiction and your child is already absorbed in the electronic world, you can still set limits. It will require more negotiation and explaining than if you had started earlier, but don't give up.

Don't fall for "All my friends can do this" because maybe they can and maybe they can't. This statement is heard in every household, and it can become a black hole for parents. The best answer is "That's not our rule at our house." The strongest defense parents have is the idea of *fair* versus *equal*. Explain that your family is not equal to other families and doesn't do things the same way as other families. Then say that fairness is important in your family and you want the rules to be as fair as possible, but you can't treat your child equally because they are different from their friends. Tell them you are committed to treating them fairly based on their maturity level, grades, and behavior.

Your electronic landscape should extend to the car, both before your child learns to drive and after. They must understand that a car is a dangerous place – thousands of pounds of moving metal in which you must make instantaneous decisions. A driver is easily distracted by texts, phone calls, plugging their iPhone into the system to play music, changing radio stations, etc. Your child is the most precious thing you have. Guard them with your life. Keeping them safe means keeping the car safe and keeping them safe in the car.

Become a Role Model

Include yourself in these guidelines. Model balanced electronics use when your child is present. If the family rule is no cell phones at the dinner table, abide by that rule yourself.

You don't have to do this alone. Talk to other parents. Urge your school, scouting group, or religious institution to host electronics education for students. Your local PTA can create a learning event for parents and students so you can learn electronics safety in a group setting. Kids need to know things like:

- Don't give your name, address, or phone number to anyone – and the reasons why this is so important.
- Passing nude pictures is child pornography, even if you are a child.
- Electronic harassment is still bullying, even if it's done virtually.
- People are more likely to hurt others' feelings when they are anonymous than when they are face to face.
- People set up fake profiles on social media and pretend to be someone they are not. This is called catfishing, and anyone they meet on the internet could be catfishing.
- Online friends are not the same as real friends.
- Online posts are not always truthful or the whole story.
- Plagiarism is a serious offense. They must follow the rules provided by their teachers for using online sources for schoolwork.
- You own their phone, computer, and gaming system, and will check their usage.
- Many websites are dangerous, can harbor viruses and spyware, and can track usage.

Check Your Guns at the Edge of Town

I have always loved westerns, especially those with John Wayne. Remember when the sheriff would say, "You gotta check your guns at the edge of town"? When cowboys checked their guns at the edge of town, they were less likely to fight.

You can apply that concept to your electronic landscape. If you feel it necessary, don't hesitate to confiscate electronics during the hours when you don't allow your child to use them. Be prepared for a fight, but there is no reason a kid needs their phone at 3:00am. They will claim they need it to wake up, but an old-fashioned alarm clock does the same thing. It did for you, and it did for me. The reason kids want to have their phones with them in the middle of the night is because they are connecting with others in different time zones or doing something inappropriate. If a teen says his girlfriend will freak out if he doesn't answer his phone in the middle of the night, tell him you will call her parents and let them know that their daughter needs more support. There is no logical reason for a teen to use their phone at home in the middle of the night.

This concept also applies to the electronic devices you use for your work. Work equipment must not be used by the children in the family, especially because you don't put the same protections on your devices that you put on your kid's devices. Let your child know that your work computer is always off limits to them. Explain that you have confidential documents on that machine that only you should access. Explain that if anything inappropriate appears on your work computer, you're in trouble and could be fired. Let them know that most employers track how company computers are used and which websites are visited.

Be sure to securely store your work computer when it's at home and that you use a very secure password to access it. Your child or one of their friends might be tempted to hack it, steal it, or cause some other problem with it. Store it securely and ensure it is backed up securely using an off-site service.

Sign out after using your work computer at home – every time! The most common mistakes are using a password that your child can figure out and forgetting to sign out when running to the bathroom or attending to a crying baby; and voilà – they have access to your work computer that has no child protections on it. Consider keeping your laptop in your locked car overnight and whenever you're not using it.

You would think that teenagers would be smarter than to use your computer because it could get you into trouble, but the teen brain is a reptilian brain. It seeks immediate gratification. It does not consider all the possible consequences of its decisions. Your child can easily make a bad decision that negatively impacts your employment.

Protect your passwords and protect your work computer. Select passwords that your child cannot guess and update them regularly. Don't store your passwords in an easily accessible location such as in your desk drawer or in a notebook you keep at your desk.

Video Game Tips

Video games can be fun and educational. They can even help kids cope with long waits at a doctor's office or sitting through their sister's dance recital. However, parents need to monitor them carefully.

The first step is to follow the guidelines and ratings provided for games just as you do with movies. If a game is marked M for Mature, it is full of violence, blood, and maybe even sexual activity. Do you want your fourth-grader playing that type of game? If your older child has them, is your younger child watching while they play? Establish firm rules for your older kids about what they can play when the younger ones are around.

Encourage playing games that are positive and growth-oriented. There is some good stuff available online. They can even participate in activities on the internet that are helpful to other people, and have a positive experience while satisfying their craving to fit in by joining the internet gaming world. You can't wrap them up and protect them from everything, but you can show them the positive side of electronics. Play as a family. Have them teach you how to play. They will love that!

Before you buy a game or allow your child to play it, research it. Go to the store and try the game. Ask the clerk for information. Read online reviews. You'll be able to determine if the game is appropriate for your child's age, developmental stage, and temperament. There are many games to choose from, so there is no need to allow your child to play games that you believe are not in their best interests, especially when they are young.

When your older teen is playing games that include online chatting, listen in occasionally. You will be surprised! If your child is playing Call of Duty or another first-person shooting game, they might be hearing other players make racial slurs, swear, and use raunchy language. Listen in regularly, and then you can talk with your adolescent about how that kind of talk makes them feel and if they think it's okay for others to speak that way. Your child will say that it is not their fault if other people use bad language, which is true, so ask them for ideas about what they should do when others are using inappropriate language. This is a valuable life skill that can be used in many settings.

Monitor Technology

As you are creating your electronic landscape with your child, make it clear that you will be checking the history on all their electronic devices. Create a firm rule that if the history on the device gets erased, you'll know they are hiding something and they will lose their electronics privileges. This simple rule is clear and easy to understand.

Be a friend with your child on every social media network. If your older teen balks at this, ask a responsible young relative of yours, like one of your nieces or nephews, to do this for you. You want to know if your child is making suicidal comments, bullying others, or posting pictures that should not be shared with the world. If you don't know how to check... google it.

Educate yourself on how you can best set up your home network to monitor the websites your child is visiting. If you don't know how to do this, ask the I.T. professional at your office, a neighbor, or an older teen from your church or temple to come over and teach you. There are many things kids know about electronics that parents don't, such as how to use a phone as a hotspot that can't be tracked, how to make a phone call from a computer, and how to access a neighbor's router. That's okay; you can ask for help and learn what you need to know. (Refer to chapter 13 for more about this.)

I like to talk to people in their twenties who work at Best Buy or are part of Best Buy's Geek Squad. They can build computers from the ground up and know this stuff cold. Don't be afraid to go to electronics stores and ask, "How do I know if my child is doing [this or that]?" It's an effective way to get information, it's free, and if you want to tip them or buy them something, you can easily show your appreciation.

If your computer crashes, be aware of things called cookies, viruses, malware, and ransomware. If your child is accessing sites that are not appropriate, they can inadvertently add these things to your computer. Be sure that you have virus protection on your computer that keeps it very safe, and that it is regularly updated. Ransomware is deadly; it can hold your information hostage. Viruses are tough; they can clean off your whole computer before you know it. Cookies report back and track your internet activity. Be aware. Be smart. Protect your systems.

Use Electronics to Your Advantage

Teenagers do not like to have to reassure their parents that they are being responsible when they are away from home with friends, or have conversations about where they are when their friends can hear that they are talking to their parents. Here is a secret from a child psychologist: text them. They will text back. Texting offers less emotion and confrontation, so it feels more comfortable to teens. It works well when you want to know where they are and the people they are with. Make it clear during your electronic-landscape discussions that if you send a text you expect them to answer it as soon as possible. You can even text them while you are both in the house, especially if you are arguing. Using text messages can help diffuse a tense situation because you are communicating in their language.

Gather the email addresses and cell phone numbers of the parents of your child's friends. It's important that you learn a bit about your child's friends and their families. Do they share your values? Do they have similar electronics rules? It can be beneficial to younger children to inform other parents of your family rules so your child is not put in a position of having to say no to a peer. For example, you can say, "Johnny can come over to play with Billy, but we have strict rules about violent video games. Can you make sure Johnny won't play them at your house?"

Remember Uncle Al

It can seem overwhelming to build your family's electronic landscape. Start simply and use your imagination. Invite your child to plan it with you and to imagine a win-win situation in which the rules you want are in place and they can use their electronics in fun and healthy ways without hassles from you. It can require several discussions or family meetings to create this landscape, and that's okay. It's good for you and your child to have conversations and practice negotiation as well as for them to learn to comply with rules.

Once you have your electronic-landscape plan, consider posting it on the fridge where everyone can see it. You can agree to review it every six months to give your child more freedom if they demonstrate responsible electronics use. If your child is working with a therapist, share it with their therapist. Update your plan regularly so it remains relevant to the age of your child. Your plan will save you many headaches, arguments, and moments of doubt. Start today to create it.

CHAPTER 9

BACK TO THE FUTURE

If you are looking to counteract or at least mitigate the circumstances associated with electronic addiction and gaming addiction, it is important to teach and encourage alternative pastimes. Remember that today's children have had little exposure to some of the things we experienced when we were their age. Depending on how young or old you are, your childhood experiences vary from mine; nevertheless the "back to the future" approach can help your child experience the real world.

What did you do for fun when you were a kid? Here's my list:

- Rode my bike
- Used my imagination to build stuff
- Played in the neighborhood
- Volunteered at the YMCA
- Wrestled
- Played soccer
- Spent time with relatives
- Dabbled in karate
- Camped in the woods
- Went fishing and took canoe trips
- Skied
- Tried lots of new things – some went well, and others did not

My family traveled. We went to Florida once a year and stayed with friends. I got a chance to see the beach, shells, Thomas Edison's workshop, and the Shell Factory in Fort Myers, and to experience a different way of living than I was accustomed to in Ohio. We also went to Canada. We went to a lodge and spent time in nature where there was no television. We went fishing, swimming, water skiing, and dealt with bugs. I had to invent things to do. I would catch frogs, dig worms for fishing, read comic books and *Mad* magazine, work on puzzles, and play board games. Our family bonded even though we had some challenges at times.

Take inventory of what you did as a kid and where you found enjoyment. What do you remember as the highlights of your life? I remember that spending time with my family in the car was fun, even though I threw up when we were on winding roads. On those car trips we had time to talk, play games, and sing along with the radio.

Kids today are so busy trying to get to the goal that they miss the journey. Don't forget the journey yourself, and take time to pause and talk with your child about how their growing-up journey is going. "The journey" means different things to different people, but it can be as simple as eating at a new restaurant – perhaps trying exotic fare, walking down an attractive street, meeting new people, understanding different walks of life, or exploring a national park. Your kids need all these experiences to grow and develop.

Parents Are Always Teachers

I learned both tangible and intangible things from my parents. Most children are exposed to life by their parents first. I could waterski when I was six. I could fish with the best of them. I knew how to run a boat. I knew those things because I watched my dad do them.

But there were intangibles, too. My dad was a very kind man, never mean to anybody, and everybody always had a kind word about him. I watched him operate with people and learned from that. He taught me fundamental people-skills that I've used all my life.

Your child will also learn about values and ethics by observing you. My father was a salesman for beauty and barber supplies, and he was one of the greatest salesmen that ever lived. He had a lot of vision, and thought about things before they happened, but did not have the confidence or planning to carry them out. My dad predicted that nail salons would be bigger than hair salons long before it happened. Unfortunately, he did not have the confidence to become a pioneer in that industry, but he certainly saw the trend. My mother, on the other hand, was very assertive. She would go for things that she wanted. She taught me about setting goals and working hard to reach them.

I took my son camping beginning when he was quite young and shared with him my love of the outdoors. Today he is planning to become a landscape architect. You never know how your example will shape your child's future. At the very least you will create positive memories and great family stories.

If you are going back to the future, take inventory of what you learned from your parents – both the tangible skills and the intangible traits that made you who you are today. What do you want your child to know when they leave your home and become an adult? Make a list of the practical skills and the values you wish to pass along. Then use activities to teach these skills.

Every time you take your child to the store or have them do the laundry, cook, run errands, or do their chores, you are teaching them valuable life skills, even if they complain. It's a wise idea to keep your child busy and doing things to contribute to the family and the community. By doing this you naturally create a balance between time spent online and time spent with people.

Here are some ideas:

- Try activities with your child that neither of you has tried before. This puts you on equal footing. Funny thing is, they are often better at it than we are because they are more agile and learn more quickly. Just try anything. Take classes together offered by the public library or the parks and recreation department. Go bowling, to the batting cages, or put up a badminton net in your backyard. What about a river-rafting trip or visiting a cave? Have some fun together and then go out for a doughnut afterward. Why a doughnut? It's not very healthy, but doughnut shops have unique atmospheres that foster conversation. Anytime you can get your teen to talk *with* you instead of your talking *at* them is time well invested.

- Go retro. I liked to take my children to local historical museums such as the Crawford Auto Museum in Cleveland or the Stan Hywet Hall manor house and gardens in Akron. While my kids were not as interested as I was, I showed them things like how people did things before there was electricity. Civil War reenactments and living history museums are also fun. Every location has local history that you can explore with your children.

- Consider volunteering together. Volunteering for a good cause makes you feel good, you help others, and you teach your child to give back to society. Volunteering comes in many packages; you can help people, animals, or even the environment. Our family delivered meals to the homeless at Christmastime. Being Jewish, it was a great time to give the Christian people a break and help people who needed it.

- Do some things that are fun, but bizarre. I loved taking my children to a bingo parlor. If you have never been to a bingo parlor, it is a world unto itself. There are serious players who play six bingo cards at once who are fun to watch. You might win something; probably not. But it's an enjoyable evening out, especially when followed by a doughnut or some ice cream.

- Learn together. Many places now offer parent/child activities such as painting, martial arts, and cooking classes.

- Explore your artsy side. Art comes in many forms. You can visit museums. I enjoyed taking my children to a paint-your-pottery place because we could create something together, talk while we were working, and take home a finished product. We created some great memories there, and you can too.

- As I wrote above, traveling offers opportunities to see things and to do things that you have not done before. It is important to include your child in the planning. Help them look up lodging, restaurants, and attractions in the area they want to visit. That way they can be a part of it.

- If you are really daring, go on an expedition off the grid such as camping, skiing, fishing, hiking, or boating. These trips allow you an opportunity to get into nature and have some family time doing novel activities. Even if you don't have the experience to teach these skills to your child, you can easily hire a guide to lead you. If your budget is limited, try exploring county and state parks. Even a day trip with a picnic lunch can be a great family experience.

- Go back in time. It can be fun to take your child to see where you grew up. Show them the houses you lived in, where your parents worked, your old schools, and the places where you had adventures or part-time jobs. This gives you an opportunity to share some of your struggles and achievements. It gives your child a picture of you as a young person so that they realize you understand what they are going through as they age.

- Make a family scrapbook. My mother made scrapbooks for me that I appreciate now that she is deceased. There are funny pictures of myself, my dog, and of some of our family experiences. It brings back a lot of good memories. Scrapbooking together is fun and captures family memories that your child will cherish in the future.

- Pick a hobby to share. Simple things work best, such as metal detecting, coin collecting, gardening, cooking, raising animals, antiquing, crafting, or stamp collecting. A friend of mine is one of the world champions in aerobatic remote-control plane competitions. He has traveled all over the world for competitions and taught his son to do it. I taught my son to camp. He is a good camper and has a great appreciation for the outdoors, and I am very proud of him for this. He worked at the Cleveland Botanical Garden, and as I mentioned wants to become a landscape architect – at least right now. I take a lot of pride in the fact that introducing him to wilderness gave us something we can share for the rest of our lives.

- Explore music together. Kids are listening to a wider variety of music than we did, thanks to the internet. I know a twenty-one-year-old boy who learned to love Frank Sinatra because he heard it all the time when he worked as a busboy at a country club. A young lady I know loves to go dancing to big band music. Your child might appreciate The Beatles, jazz, classical music, or 1980s hair bands like Boston and Journey. Tell them about vinyl records, eight-tracks, and cassettes. Point them out at thrift stores. Play a variety of music in your home, even if it comes from your computer, and listen to it together. When you find music that your child enjoys, attend a concert or symphony performance. Even watching high school marching bands at football games and local parades exposes your child to new styles of music. My son is named Chapin, after the folk singer Harry Chapin. He knows his namesake's music and why it inspired my wife and me. Music is something we share even if it's me listening to what my children like to show respect for their choices, as they respect mine.

When your child has a problem, don't give them the answer; use *collaborative problem-solving*, which is stopping and thinking about it. Anybody old enough to remember the TV show *Columbo* remembers how he would ask leading or tricky questions. Rather than telling your child what to do, ask, "How can we fix this? What might be a better thing to do?"

Share some "going back in time" experiences with your child to distract them from being online and to create lasting memories.

Don't Neglect the Future

The flip side is the future part. Have your child teach you about electronics or video games. You can explore new apps, new programs, and let your child be your teacher, which is powerful for their self-esteem. Like me, you might not have a strong interest in the video games, but I still enjoy learning about them from my children. You can have fun laughing together and let them enjoy being more adept than their parent. In this way they are at least interacting with someone while they are using electronics. You can play video games with them for a little bit and balance that by saying, "I will play video games with you for now if you come with me to the hardware store later."

You can also explore the future by visiting science or space museums or attending lectures about aspects of the future that interest your child. Try going to a movie theatre to watch a science fiction film and then talking about what your child predicts will happen in the future over pizza.

Going into the future also means learning some of their words for things. The other night I asked my eighteen-year-old daughter, "Hmm, does somebody have a crush on somebody?" She said, "Dad, you're so old school. Nobody has a crush anymore – *crush* is not the word." We laughed, and she taught me terms like *BFF* (best friends forever) and *friends with benefits* (blech – *that's really inappropriate in my opinion*) and other terms teens use that I don't know. Again, it put her in the role of teacher, which balances all the times I try to teach her things.

Take time to explore back to the future. Take your children down your Memory Lane and let them take you down their Memory Lane. Share information. Share funny stories of how you and your spouse met. Share funny stories about your past. Have fun with back to the future.

CHAPTER 10

IT'S ALL ABOUT OTHERS - SOCIAL AND FRIENDSHIP SKILLS

Does it ever feel like you are a visitor in a strange land when you are talking to your child about electronics? Today's youth grew up with a cell phone in their hand and the world of the internet at their fingertips. We parents began our electronics use as adults, probably at work. Remember word processors and early computer programs that made life easier? Before that it was the typewriter. Thank goodness there was a home computer by the time I did my dissertation! For most adults, electronics are both a work tool and a source of entertainment.

Our kids have a different viewpoint. Electronics provide them with constant entertainment, easy access to information, and shortcuts to everyday tasks. Kids may forget to brush their teeth, but they never forget to check their phones and social media accounts daily, often hourly. Some kids are so connected to their electronics that they panic when they are not permitted to use them. Because they spend so much time online, many lack the vital social and friendship skills that make life function in the non-electronic world.

In a nutshell, social skills help people relate to one another for fun and for more vital pursuits like getting a job and career networking – crucial skills in today's society. Consider job hunting. Most jobs are filled through networking. If your child has no network of friends, it's difficult for them to hear about job opportunities, both as a youth and in adulthood.

Social skills include things like disagreeing appropriately, taking turns, and assertiveness (see the detailed list in the next section). They include both verbal and non-verbal skills, and are often learned from observation and experience. If kids are not observing and experiencing relationships with others because they are spending the bulk of their time online, problems will develop.

I offer fifteen different social-skills training groups in my practice. Social skills are essential for success in the world, but many people are challenged by them. They can be challenged because of learning disabilities, autism, shyness, or just too much time online. Whatever the reason, there are things that parents can do at home to foster the development of solid social skills.

Assessing Social Skills

There are many ways to measure and assess social skills. Your child's teacher or therapist might be able to provide some printed assessments. (For a free, helpful social-skills assessment, visit http://CenterForElectronicAddiction.com.) A good rule of thumb is to notice how your child interacts with others – both peers and adults – and measure that behavior against what you observe in other kids.

Look for the skills listed below. I labeled a few "Vital Skills" because they are important building blocks for further social development and later intimacy.

For elementary-school-aged children:

- Listen to others
- Follow instructions
- Obey rules at home and school
- Ask for help
- Make eye contact
- Take turns
- Win or lose without an explosion or taunting
- Respond positively to good-natured teasing
- Play and talk pleasantly with a peer
- Engage in group activities and conversations
- Interact respectfully with adults such as grandparents and coaches
- Offer help
- VITAL SKILL: Awareness of others' feelings and how to react to them appropriately
- VITAL SKILL: Using words to describe feelings

For adolescents:

- All the items in the previous list
- Resolve conflicts peacefully
- Start and maintain conversations with peers and adults
- Give and receive compliments
- Set and reach personal goals
- Be assertive but not aggressive

- Make purchases in the community
- Show awareness of personal strengths and weaknesses
- Employ empathy in response to others' emotions
- Recognize and discuss complex emotions such as frustration, shame, and embarrassment
- Read social cues, and both obvious and subtle facial expressions
- Maintain positive relationships with at least a small group of friends
- Understand the difference between acquaintances and true friends
- Avoid doing things that hurt others
- Apologize and make amends for relationship mistakes
- VITAL SKILL: Give and receive emotional support in relationships with close friends

Teaching Friendship Skills

When you were growing up you found friends in the neighborhood, at school, in sports or community activities like scouting, or in a religious organization. It probably didn't seem like a big deal; you just found someone you liked, began doing things together, and became friends. Of course, there were some friendships that didn't work out or last long, but you probably didn't need to be taught how to make friends. In most situations your parents knew your classmates' parents or could contact them via a school directory if they wanted to meet them.

Life is not as simple for our kids today. Many mistake online friends for true friends. There are dangerous people even in our own neighborhoods, so kids don't spend as much time playing outdoors without parental supervision.

In the social-skills groups I lead at my office, we spend most of the time talking about friendships. When I ask individuals about their friends, they tell me about their online friendships. I don't suggest to them, or to you, that online friendships are bad; instead I talk about the differences between the three types of friendships below:

- **Acquaintance friend:** This is someone you know personally from school, church, camp, or your community. You know each other's names and say hello when you see each other. This person seems friendly, but you have not gotten to know them well yet. For example, you might sit with them at lunch.
- **Friend-friend:** This is a friend with whom you engage in activities such as going to the movies, sleepovers, attending sporting events, or visiting each other's homes. You trust this person and know them better than an acquaintance friend.
- **Online friend:** This is someone who shares your interests, but you have not met them personally and don't really know what they are like in the offline world.

Today's kids struggle with friend-friend relationships. They base their friendships on shared interests. If they know someone who lives nearby but don't believe they have any shared interests, they won't try to initiate a friendship because there are so many opportunities to find people with those interests online.

When Friendship Goes Wrong

I know a young lady – I'll call her Beth – who had two friends from school. One was in the hospital after a suicide attempt.

Beth called her hospitalized friend with her other friend muted on the line, told her that the other girl was not her friend, and gave specific examples of betrayals. Beth felt like she was doing the girl in the hospital a favor, not realizing how cruel her actions were to everyone. Now, none of them are friends.

A teenaged girl came to my office after her so-called friend posted a photo online of her wearing stained pants after she unexpectedly got her period at school. She was mortified and didn't want to return to that school.

Many young people struggle with friendships because they lack social skills and empathy for others. For others it's because their brains are not wired to think of the impact of their behavior on others – they just aren't thinking about it. This is an issue for both boys and girls, but it manifests differently in each gender.

Girls are motivated by being popular and fitting in. They use social media to follow the girls they believe are the most popular in their schools – the "A-listers," as it were. Some will do anything to become friends with the A-listers, including bullying less popular girls on social media. They can believe that to be popular means excluding or belittling others.

If you have a daughter, talk to her about the "popular girls" and discuss whether they are good potential friends. To spark a discussion about cruel behavior, consider watching the movie *Mean Girls* or other age-appropriate films about cruelty in school, and discuss the film with your daughter.

Boys also struggle with friendships, but don't always seek popularity. Many avoid boys they feel are more powerful than they are. A shy boy would rather isolate himself than take on jocks or others whom they believe act superior in some way. Boys are more likely to isolate themselves and give up on friendships than risk being hurt or humiliated.

Is Your Child the Problem?

If your child receives no invitations from other kids, it is a signal that they might be having trouble with friendship skills. Observe your child in social situations. Do peers greet them? Do they greet them back? Everyone is invited to birthday parties when they are little, but this changes in upper elementary school, and that's when you can assess whether your child is getting invitations. When you observe your child interacting with others, do they:

- Know how to start a conversation, or just sit silently?
- Take turns?
- Share?
- Ask others what activities they would enjoy doing?
- Engage, or withdraw?
- Act in a way that is annoying or bothersome?

If your child is not included in social situations, what seems to be the reason?

If you can see that your child is having trouble with friendships, do everything you can to teach them how to be a good friend. When you're watching television or a movie together, point out how friends in the story resolve differences or work together. Talk about the differences between the types of friendship listed above, and how having a friend-friend can be a wonderful thing. Tell stories about your own friends at the dinner table and how you got to know and like them. Take your child to the mall and watch people at the food court. See what your child notices about other kids their age and how they relate to others. I call this being a "social spy." It's fun and is a non-threatening activity for kids who are shy or isolated.

Talk about how people are all different: Some thrive with lots of friends while others are happier with just one or two close friends. Assure your child that you don't expect them to be popular or to like everyone else, but that life is better when they have friends to share it with, including friends they see regularly. Send the message that even though your child's style might be different from others', it is not bad, and that life will be much more enjoyable with friends.

It is important not to let your child isolate themselves at home. Many need parental encouragement to engage in social activities because their isolation at home is familiar and comfortable. If your child does not respond positively to your encouragement, seek out a therapist who can help you teach them social skills and uncover the underlying issues.

Parents can tell when their children are having social challenges. You'll observe that your child doesn't do anything with peers and doesn't want to invite anyone to your house. There might be comments from school personnel about your child not getting along well with others, struggling in groups, or defying authority. If this sounds like your child, it's important to teach them about friendships as soon as possible.

Establishing Offline Friendships

Psychologists use the term *successive approximation*, which means getting people to move in the direction of a goal in small steps, getting successively closer to it. It is important to know that social skills develop along a continuum. You will not be able to take an isolated, socially awkward individual and transform them overnight into someone with lots of friends. However, you can use the steps below to begin the process and help your child learn to find and keep a friend in the real world while maintaining their online relationships. Remember the concept of *balanced use of electronics*. There is no need to demand that your child give up their online friends; instead, try to foster a few local friendships and balance those with time online so your child has opportunities to learn relationship skills.

1. Encourage your child to identify someone who could become their friend from those they already have contact with in their daily life. This could be someone from school, church, or scouting; a neighbor; or even someone they met at a gaming event at the video store.

2. The next step is for your child to get their name, email address, gamer tag, phone number, and/or social media contact information.

3. If your child is young, take the initiative and set up a time for the kids to get together in person.

4. If you have a teenager, help them think of an activity both would enjoy and then coach your child to make the invitation. Consider activities that don't require lots of conversation such as swimming, bowling, going to the movies, or even going to an arcade.

5. Help them with how to ask and how to be an acquaintance first – how to give the person your number first and get their number when they call. Explain that it's not polite to ask someone for their number who did not offer it themselves, or to ask a third party for someone else's number.

6. Praise your child for making the invitation and then attending the event. This is a big risk for someone who lacks friendship skills.

You might be wondering why I suggested a visit to an arcade. It might seem counterintuitive, but when people play arcade games together they are engaging in *parallel play*, which is a step in developing friendships. Parallel play allows shy kids to interact with someone but does not require much negotiation, sharing, or conversation. It's a way to dip their toe into the water of an offline relationship without much pressure. If that event goes well, follow it up with an activity that requires more interaction such as playing board games, attending a ball game, or going bowling.

Once your child has completed this step, discuss it together. Ask if they had fun, what they liked, what they didn't enjoy, and if they would like to get to know the other person better to see if they could become a friend-friend. If it did not go well, explain that we don't always click with everyone we meet, and talk about who else might be a potential friend. Try to figure out what went wrong; then help them make changes.

You might need to teach your child how to respond appropriately when a potential friendship does not work out. Monitor your child to see if they respond to invitations from others. Some of my clients are over-eager to become friends and send the potential friend multiple texts every day, which of course can result in being rejected. Others feel frightened and do not respond to subsequent messages and invitations. After a few requests have been ignored, kids give up, just as adults do.

Relating to Adults

Social skills do not encompass only friendships with peers; they include the ability to ask for help, make purchases, order at restaurants, respond to authority figures, and set appropriate boundaries. Kids learn these skills via direct experiences, and in small, comfortable steps.

I know a thirty-year-old woman who lives at home with her parents and relies on them for all her social interactions. After many years of electronic isolationism, her patterns are very hard to break. Whenever you can, encourage your child to interact with people. Don't always order clothing online; instead, take them to a store and have them ask the clerk for help. Encourage kids to place orders at restaurants instead of speaking for them. When it's appropriate for their age, have them run errands to pick up dry cleaning or get a few things at the grocery store.

Attend school sporting events. Scores don't count; the social exposure does. Many kids don't like sports and don't even know the score when they're at a high school football game; they are there for social reasons.

As mentioned above, consider opportunities for volunteering. Many of my clients love animals and feel more comfortable with them than they do with people, so they volunteer at an animal shelter. Volunteering can be a precursor to a part-time job, which is another great place to learn social skills. If you can, volunteer as a family to work the concession stand at a school sporting event. It will be a good opportunity to observe your child in a social setting interacting with peers. You might spot a potential friend or uncover a challenging behavior.

Finding Social-Skills Training

If your child has deficits in social skills, they will certainly benefit from a social-skills group facilitated by a professional therapist who has experience with youth groups. Talk to the school counselor about social-skills groups provided by the school, whether after school by an outside therapist or during the school day by school personnel. Find as many resources as you can to support your child's social development. Consider it tutoring for real life.

The best option is a group that includes peers in a similar developmental stage so that your child will fit into the conversation. Some therapists cluster kids in groups in which they share a similar diagnosis as well, such as a group for those who struggle with depression, have ADHD, or abuse substances.

It is highly likely that your child will fight you over attending a group program. It's scary for most kids to enter a new group, and especially one led by a therapist. Be prepared for arguments. My suggestion is to be very honest and say, "I'm concerned that you are having a hard time relating to people and making friends. Let's both go to see Dr. X and see what she can recommend to help." Then the therapist can assess the challenges and discuss group options with you and your child, and the three of you can decide together what would be most helpful.

CHAPTER 11

CREATING AN INTERVENTION PLAN

One of my former clients was absolutely brilliant at computer coding. He loved it and wanted to spend every moment on his computer. Thankfully his parents noticed that his love of computers was compromising his social and emotional development. They pushed for him to attend therapy and participate in social-skills groups. They also taught him to keep a balance in his life. Today this young man is living in Silicon Valley and has a very successful career in computer coding. He also has a satisfying personal life and can live as he wishes. He did not need to give up his electronics, just learn to use them in a healthy and balanced fashion.

That's the best goal for youths with electronic addiction. Abstinence from electronics is impossible. Healthy, balanced use is very possible, especially when parents intervene knowledgably. I don't suggest punishing your child for using computers. Instead, talk with them, reinforce your electronic landscape, and offer praise and rewards when those limits are kept. There might be times when your child needs to face consequences for breaking the family electronic landscape, but that is not the place to begin.

Start Early

All kids can benefit from a balance of healthy activities alongside their use of electronics. It's essential for parents to stress good nutrition, exercise, outdoor activities, and time spent interacting with others. Beyond sampling the activities suggested in chapter 9, if you can make non-computer time as fun and rewarding as time spent online you'll be well on your way to helping your child create a natural balance.

By now you are familiar with the signs of electronic addiction and may see them in your child. It's hard to pinpoint when an electronic addiction begins, as electronics are so woven into our lives. Like autism, anxiety, depression, and other mental health issues, the earlier the better when beginning intervention. Once habits become entrenched, intervention gets more and more difficult.

If you observe some of these early warning signs, your child needs help learning to use electronics wisely:

- Overuse of electronics
- Lack of real-world friendships
- Temper tantrums when asked to get off the internet
- Moods that are linked to success at playing games or responses to social media posts
- Too much anticipation of the next game
- You hear from others that your child might be addicted
- Loss of their online group of friends
- Wanting to come right home after school to get online
- Not wanting to go places – even out to eat with the family (this is a big warning sign and should alert parents to action)
- Getting bored easily

Early intervention includes:

- Recognition of the problem
- Managing the problem for your young child until they can manage it themselves
- Joining a social-skills group
- Increasing social interactions
- Creating a well-rounded social program
- Seeking professional help, even if only you attend.* (Sometimes parents can benefit from therapy without their child present. It's okay to ask for parenting help.)
- Have trusted relatives speak to your child. (Parents are ignorant in their teen's eyes!)

* I recommend cognitive behavioral therapy, which helps individuals identify their thinking patterns and change them, leading to more positive behavior. This form of therapy is proved to be successful for people with addiction challenges and is suitable for children and adults. (You'll read more about how to find a good therapist to help your child in chapter 15.)

Remember that electronic addiction tends to stunt developmental growth. This means that although kids can be intellectually stimulated by learning information on the internet or by the thrills of their games, they can be socially or emotionally stunted because experiences with peers are limited. Signs of emotional stunting include:

- Rage, violence, or tantrums when asked to stop using electronics
- Lack of empathy; for example, staying glued to a cell phone instead of conversing with guests

- Using a parent's or grandparent's credit card to fund electronic purchases
- Inability to socialize with peers in an age-appropriate manner
- Inability to relate to siblings and/or pets
- Telling jokes that are immature for their age
- Seeking to be with adults or younger peers rather than peers of the same age. Many kids who experience delays in their social and emotional development find it easier to socialize with adults and younger peers. Youngsters are usually thrilled to have an older child pay attention to them. Older adults are generally kind to and accepting of quirky kids. Socializing with these people is safe and easy. If your child avoids interacting with others of their age, there is a problem to address.

It Takes a Village

It's challenging to help your child learn to balance their use of electronics and can create havoc in a house and in a marriage. Use the ideas in this book and the information you glean from your child's therapist to create an *intervention plan* that works for you and your child.

In some cases, parental behavior contributes to the development of electronic addiction. Be sure you're not sending mixed messages to your child by being tethered to your own cell phone or gaming systems while you're asking them to curb their use.

It is important for parents to present a united front. Both Mom and Dad need to be involved in creating the intervention plan and enforcing it consistently. This is a challenge for all parents, but especially when the child spends time in two different households. Do your best to ensure that all parents are on the same page. Get grandparents and step-parents involved as well. I call this the "all hands on deck" system. If one adult in your child's life does not comply with your intervention plan, it will fail. Inconsistency is the route to an oppositional, defiant child.

Children who are addicted to drugs and/or alcohol, as well as those with electronic addiction, often exhibit the behaviors of *oppositional defiant disorder* (discussed in chapter 6). Oppositional defiant behavior is all about control. The more you fight your child for control, the more they will try to grab control from you. Expect that your child will try to resist the limits you place on electronics use, but do not fight force with force. Be calm; set limits; and walk away, having established pre-set ways to enforce limits. Don't throw the book at them when they fail to obey rules, but calmly enforce them per the intervention plan you set up as a family. Parents can get angry and say things like "You'll never see your video games again" or another non-enforceable consequence. All consequences need to be enforceable.

Of course, if your child is older they will go to a friend's house or the library to play video games. Libraries have their own regulations, and library personnel often police computer use. But libraries usually provide wireless access, so kids can use their devices at or near a library without supervision. Find out what the rules are at your child's friends' homes, whether your child is monitored there, and where your child can access wireless internet service without supervision.

As already mentioned, your child is going to hate this. They're going to say that nobody else's parents check with anybody else's parents; that you are overprotective; blah blah blah. Resist the temptation to give in. You are the parent; you make the decisions. If there is no supervision at your child's friend's home, then maybe your child should not go there. Find the weak spots in your plan to head off problems at the pass, or your intervention will fail.

Consider help from your "village" before confronting your child about electronic addiction. Get all the adults on board first, then maintain regular communication with your team of adults so they know what's going well and where the struggles are. This will help everyone enforce the intervention plan and communicate to your child the same message about healthy, balanced use. If one of the adults involved doesn't treat this as a serious issue, give them a copy of this book! You can discuss rules and modify them as needed, just don't be pressured into it. Here are some guiding thoughts:

- Some rules are negotiable; some are not.
- As your child matures emotionally, the rules can be adjusted. *Emotional* maturity is the key, as opposed to chronological age, especially for social media access!
- Do not make unilateral decisions. Consult the other adults in your child's life.
- Exceptions can be made if discussed *in advance*. For example, for a treat you might suspend the rules when your child's school takes a snow day.
- Don't make rash, on-the-spot decisions; stick with the plan.

Your Ultimate Goal

The goal of all the interventions I discuss in this book is to help kids learn how to manage their behavior and use electronics in a healthy way. They are not born with this skill. By the way, neither are adults. We need practice too, and make mistakes. And progress varies. Sometimes you think the problem is solved only to have it flare up again unexpectedly. In my twenty-five years as a therapist I've learned that all intervention plans need to have:

- Clear expectations and simple rules designed with some ongoing input from the child
- Rewards set in advance for meeting expectations
- Consequences set in advance for not following the rules
- Consistency in enforcement on the part of all the adults involved
- Consideration of the needs and issues of the individual child. Some kids can regulate their behavior while others cannot. If your child has ADHD or another developmental issue, they will probably require more parental support and instruction than others would to meet your plan's expectations.
- Regular discussions about how things are going, including praise for effort
- Timelines for reevaluating and loosening boundaries if progress has been made
- A recovery plan for when your child fails to comply so that relationships are maintained

Begin with an honest discussion with your child. Tell the truth. Say that you are concerned that your child is addicted to electronics and you want to help them learn to use them appropriately. Give concrete examples. Then ask your child to help you create the intervention plan. Include things like:

- Times when and places where electronics may be used
- Where electronics are to be stored when they are not in use
- The types of games, apps, media, and sites your child can visit

I was on vacation recently and observed an adolescent girl and her father eating breakfast together. The young lady was furiously texting on her phone and appeared to be angry. Her father said, "I know you're mad at your mom, but you're taking it out on me. I came here to be with you and not to watch you text." She did not put down her phone, so he got up and left the table. When you are setting boundaries, remember to include separate rules for vacations and review them with your child before the trip. Kids often assume that when they are away from home all the rules go out the window. It's important to always talk about your expectations before any change in routine.

Once your intervention plan is in place, it is important to remind your child that they are always making choices. If they choose not to follow a family rule, they will not be punished but will *experience the consequences of their choice.* Communicate this clearly and consistently. Use this template: "You know you need to do your homework before getting online, and you chose not to do that. That was your choice, so now you won't have access to your games tonight." When you stress that your child knew the rules in advance and made a different choice, it helps them see that they can either earn a reward or not, based on their choices. This will help you cut down on arguments.

Many kids try to manipulate the plan and torment you to get more screen time. You may have given in to whining in the past regarding other kinds of rules, and your child is going to test you to see how firmly you will stand by the expectations of the intervention. Use the *response cost* method. Tell your child, "I've said no and that means no. If you bug me about this again today, you will lose [X]," inserting a consequence that will motivate your child to stop complaining. However, if you say it, you must stick to it, so stay calm and employ consequences that you can enforce. Telling them that they will never see their cell phone again is not a reasonable consequence.

Some children can't effectively manage their behavior and need shorter time intervals to be successful than other children. For some, ten minutes is as long as they can be expected to maintain discipline. Work with your child's therapist to create a reasonable expectation for your child's age and developmental stage. Don't give in and don't allow your child to bully you.

(In my practice I offer coaching for parents by phone. If you need coaching, call my office for an appointment at 216.292.7170 or visit http://CenterForElectronicAddiction.com.)

Create an Imbalance

Parents who bring their children to my office for therapy are seeking change, while their child doesn't mind the situation and doesn't see why a change is needed. Most kids think parents are the issue. It's my job to help the parents create an imbalance in the current situation. One approach is to create a reward system in which your child gets what they want as a reward for complying with the intervention plan. Another approach is to create a subtraction system in which your child no longer gets what they want unless they comply with the plan. For example, when a boy refuses to shower, his parents can tell him that he is not allowed to ride in the family car if he smells bad. That might mean he has to walk to school or ride his bike. As soon as he changes his behavior and showers, he is allowed back in the family car. Give your child the perception of controlling the situation, in the same way choice was discussed above.

Both approaches work well. I recommend starting with a reward system because it is the most pleasant for everyone involved. If your child does not respond well to a reward system, then it's time to start subtracting things. There are many ways to create reward and subtraction plans. Here are two of my favorite methods:

- **Pay to Play – A Reward Imbalance:** This method employs electronics use as a reward for completing chores or homework and for making efforts to increase socialization with peers. For example, if your child is allowed to play video games for two hours on Saturday afternoons without working for it, you can reward them with additional game time if they invite a classmate over or attend a school activity. This can be extended to going to a school sporting event, trying a new activity, working out, and so on.

For this method to work it must first be clear when electronics use is permitted. Consider this as an allowance. Your child can predict that they will be able to use electronics at specified times. Extra time is a bonus to be earned by spending more time with people and on offline activities. If your child is very isolated, you might need to propose the activity and support them in trying it.

- **"Amish Paradise" – A Subtraction Imbalance:** "Amish Paradise" is a substantial intervention and should not be attempted without extensive discussions with your child about boundaries and expectations. And it's not a slur about Amish people; the name is just an easy way to refer to a lifestyle without electronics. It includes serious consequences and upsets children who are addicted to their electronics, usually resulting in a lot of drama.

If your child continues to violate the rules for electronics use, warn them that one more infraction will send them to Amish Paradise for twenty-four hours. That means that they will have no access to any electronics at all – no cell phone, laptop, iPod, or gaming system. Be ready to enforce this firmly or it will not work.

Spell out this approach clearly in your intervention plan if it becomes necessary. Determine where you will store your child's electronic devices – as suggested above, in your car is usually a good place, with your keys in your pocket. If your child will be home alone after school and needs their phone for emergencies, employ the consequence during the weekend, and stick with your child during that time. You don't need to make the day horrible, so take your child with you to run errands or do yard work. Keep them busy.

Your child will feel like they are cut off and will miss something vitally important if they cannot connect with their online world. Some become frightened and cover up their fear with angry outbursts. One of my clients punched a hole in his bedroom wall. Another threatened her younger brother if he would not let her use his phone. If you fear that your child will become violent, consider taking them to a motel or cabin away from the rest of the family.

Shut down all access during the time of Amish Paradise, ensuring that your child cannot use someone else's phone. Even if you are Facebook friends with your child, they can create another Facebook account that you don't know about. Kids can be quite brilliant when it comes to getting around rules, and the online world is always evolving. By the time this book is published there might be a new way for kids to connect electronically, so stay alert to new developments.

Talk about trust with your child. Say, "If you find a way to get online without my knowing it, then I cannot trust you." If you have a young child, tell them that you cannot trust them to stay home alone while you pick up their brother or sister from dance class, so they'll have to come along. Make it their problem.

The goal of Amish Paradise is to create a strong consequence that encourages compliance with the intervention plan in the future. A side benefit is that it clearly illustrates to both you and your child that your child is addicted to electronics if they cannot go without them for a twenty-four-hour period.

I hope that you don't need to use Amish Paradise, but if you do, know that you are taking an active stand for the health of your child. This is an intervention to help, not to punish. It can be a very useful response for a kid who just won't listen or meet your expectations about electronics use. If you are working with a therapist, be sure to involve them in this process. (For more information about therapy and parental coaching, see chapter 15.)

Self-Awareness and Regulation

There are many actions you can take to help your child use electronics in a healthy way. In the end, you are teaching them how to be aware of their behavior and to regulate it. This is an important developmental task for all youths. You would not let your child eat cookies all day, neglect showers, or stay up until 4:00am on a school night. From early on it comes naturally to teach your child that everything has a start and a stop, even their favorite things. Overeating cookies has immediate consequences like getting a stomach ache, while the consequences of overuse of electronics are subtler. You know that kids will try something just because you said no – it's their nature – so it's up to you to point out the consequences.

When they first start using electronic devices, regulate their use until they develop the ability to self-regulate. It's a process that requires time and effort, but the result is a child who can use electronics in a safe and healthy way while maintaining positive relationships in the real world. By helping your child learn these skills you are giving them a healthy and positive future. It's well worth it.

The goal is to help your child learn to manage their electronics use – and their behavior in general – independently as an adult. I know a college student who could not get out of bed in time for class. His mother paid his roommate to wake him up every day. This might sound like a clever solution, but what will that young man do when his roommate is not around? As your child demonstrates more responsibility and growth, gradually provide opportunities for them to regulate their own behavior. Even if they fail miserably at first, it's an ongoing learning experience. It's your job to teach your child to manage themselves and their electronics use over time and with practice.

CHAPTER 12

STAY UP TO DATE WITH TECHNOLOGY

Matt Burk of Burk Tech is my technical director, friend, and fellow parent. Although we have a similar last name, we are not related. He's my go-to guy for keeping abreast of the latest technical advances and the ways that kids can work around their parents online. Matt and I sat down to talk about the technical aspects of what parents need to know, and I share much of what we talked about in the following chapters.

Things are always changing, and kids evolve right along with the latest technology. For example, there was a very popular cell phone app called Kix that allowed users to send text messages that were not tracked in their message folder. This was a great way for kids to have conversations via text that their parents could not see. Unfortunately, it filled up with false profiles and predators – a very dangerous place. It's not popular anymore, and most parents have never heard of it. It's a great example of how quickly technology changes.

Ten years ago parents only needed to check the browsing history on the family computer to see where their children had been online. It's harder today. Now kids don't spend a lot of time on computers. They use tablets, cell phones, iPods, and gaming systems to access the internet. Matt's son plays video games with a boy from Australia using headphones to talk with him while they play. It's incredible that two boys who live so far apart can be friends.

However, it is very easy for adults to set up fake profiles on gaming systems, social media, and websites to lure naive kids into danger. A predator sets up a fake profile pretending to be a thirteen-year-old gamer, connecting with all sorts of kids until the predator finds one in their local area, and then sets up a time to meet in person. It's easy and very scary.

One of the best ways to do this is via YouTube videos. Kids watch YouTube videos much more than television these days – it's a big part of their lives. You can do a search on "internet safety" on YouTube and come up with more than 100,000 videos just for teenagers. There are also videos for elementary students and tweens. Watch some of these videos yourself and then select ones to watch with your child. This is an excellent way to teach them about safety without having to lecture and risk being tuned out. Watching someone their age getting into a risky situation helps kids understand that there are real dangers in our world. They believe things online more readily than what you tell them, so use that to your advantage.

For example, there is an excellent video on YouTube by Coby Persin about predators on social media. He set up a fake profile on Facebook posing as a fifteen-year-old boy. With their parents' permission he friended three tween girls and set up scenarios common among predators. One girl met him at a park, another invited him to her house when her parents were gone, and the third got into his van at night. It is frightening to watch these dramatic situations that clearly illustrate how easy it is to slip into a dangerous situation. See the video at https://www.youtube.com/watch?v=6jMhMVEjEQg.

Matt recommends that you regularly watch these kinds of videos with your child and follow them with discussion. Tell your child that they should always come to you when they are scared or in a situation that seems questionable or confusing. Tell them that they won't get into as much trouble if they come to you than they would if you discover a problem on your own. Matt says, "I believe kids learn best by making mistakes. Your children will make mistakes online no matter what you do. If you can be the safe person for your child to talk with after a small mistake, you can help them learn and avoid dangerous situations."

Use Technology to Help

Matt recommends using common tools to reinforce your family's electronic landscape. Most cell phone plans include an option for bandwidth restriction for a small monthly fee. Matt pays his cell provider an extra five dollars each month for this service. It allows him to give his son a set amount of bandwidth each month, ensuring that his son doesn't gobble up the bandwidth and that other family members get the shares they need.

Cell phone providers also offer parental controls. Matt has his son's phone set so that no data can be used after 9:30 on school nights. That means that his son can't make calls, text, or surf the internet after that time. He can call 911 or his parents in case of emergency, but that's all he can do.

You can also create a firewall on your home computer network. There are several devices on the market that are easy to set up, and some internet providers offer this service. A firewall allows you to see where your child is going online and how long they spend at each website, and shut off internet access at prescribed times on prescribed days. They can still play games from a DVD, but they will not be able to "group play" with others online after the hours you have determined for their internet access.

Communication Is Key

According to Matt, communication is the most effective tool for parents who care about youth safety online. Talk to your child regularly about internet safety and healthy electronics use. Remind them that you provide them with a cell phone and other electronic devices, which is a *privilege*, and that you are responsible for helping them use these devices safely. Inform them that you will be checking their phones and other devices regularly. Then do it. Look at texts, videos, and photos to ensure there isn't anything dangerous going on.

Check firewall logs and let your child know that you will be doing so regularly. Just imagine saying, "I see you were on YouTube for twenty minutes last night. Did you find any good videos?"

Also look at the apps on your child's phone. If there is an app you are not familiar with, google it. Apps come and go quickly, so it is important to monitor them regularly just to be sure they are not dangerous.

Your child will hate this and accuse you of being harsh and controlling. That's okay. They are young and don't realize the potential danger of the online world. Their brains have not developed enough to realize that people are not always who they say they are online.

It is also important that you know the passwords to your child's phone, devices, email accounts, and social media accounts. Connect with all their accounts on Facebook, Instagram, and other social media sites so they know you see what they share online. If you have a younger relative like a niece or nephew, ask them to connect with your child on social media and alert you if they see anything that could be a problem, such as photos of parties with drinking or drugs, posts that reveal your home address or phone numbers, or bullying.

Teach your child not to reveal information that could invite robbers or predators. Posting photos of family vacations or that reveal that kids are home alone invites problems. It's fine to share vacation photos but teach your child to post them only after you are back from the trip. It may seem like a little thing, but sharing your family's whereabouts puts everyone in the family at risk.

I asked Matt how he has conversations with his kids about sex trafficking, online predators, and robbers without scaring them. He said, "I don't pull any punches with my kids. I talk to them honestly about the reality of the online world. It's better for them to be a little scared and cautious if that keeps them safe."

When I asked Matt about the dark web, he chuckled and said that he believes the entire internet is a dark and dirty place. It is full of scammers, viruses, and people with evil intentions, side by side with all the positive information. Adults and kids are at risk every time they go online, and if you tell a kid not to do something, chances are they will try to do that very thing. We did this with our parents, and our children are no different. (For more on the dark web, see chapter 13.)

Knowledge is power. Matt believes that when you teach your child about the good and bad sides of electronic communication they will be able to use it more wisely. He shared a story from the cartoon *Dragon Ball*. The main character, Goku, failed regularly, but always got back up stronger. This is a beautiful message for our kids. When they fail – and they will because they are young – remind them that they can learn from the experience and be stronger and smarter on the other side of it.

Kids Adapt Faster than Adults

Matt also reminded me that technology is always moving and growing. Kids talk to each other. When one young person finds a new computer hack or way around parental controls, they share it with all their friends. It's impossible for parents to stay on top of all these new advances. Instead of trying to do so in a vacuum, Matt urges you to make your child your ally and to work with them in a collaborative way to help them enjoy using electronics safely. Keep the lines of communication open and talk regularly about both the pros and cons of the online world. Take the role of coach and mentor so that your child can come to you with questions or concerns. That's the best tech hack of all: old-fashioned communication!

CHAPTER 13

SAFETY AND ETHICS IN THE ELECTRONIC WORLD

In January of 2017 sixteen-year-old honor-roll student Corey Walgren committed suicide after being confronted at school about an audio recording he made while having intercourse with a classmate. According to the *Chicago Sun-Times*, Corey was called in to the dean's office where the dean and school police officer confiscated his phone and found the audio as well as some partially nude photos. Corey said those photos were sent to him by others. It seems the police officer was trying to make the seriousness of the situation clear and told Corey he could be charged with child pornography and must register as a sex offender. While Corey's mother was on her way to the school, Corey left the office and jumped off a five-story parking garage to his death. You can read the full story here: https://chicago.suntimes.com/chicago-politics/naperville-teens-suicide-shows-difficulties-for-schools-on-sex-videos.

This horrific story is just one example of the dangers faced by our youth. Most have little idea how to navigate the electronic world safely, even if they are honor students. We've given them a Pandora's box with many good things in it, but also some very dangerous temptations.

It's important that parents take the lead in ensuring that their kids learn about electronic safety. Schools provide some instruction about this, but nothing can substitute for ongoing safety and ethics instruction at home. Don't assume that these issues are just for teens. Start to teach cyber safety as soon as your child begins to use electronics.

The Family Online Safety Institute recommends you start searching for websites with your child during their elementary years and show them the difference between trustworthy and unreliable websites. Talk about fake news and sham sites as a family, and help your child learn to recognize red flags and discover who is supplying the information on the website.

In July of 2017 Google launched a free online resource for parents and educators at https://beinternetawesome. withgoogle.com. This site has terrific resources for young children, including an interactive game called Internet Awesome that helps them learn how to use the internet safely.

If you have a child with special needs, there are helpful resources at https://www.fosi.org/good-digital-parenting/ autism-spectrum-disorder-parenting-guidelines.

It may seem ironic that I'm sending you to the internet to teach your child about internet safety and ethics; however, that is the best place to find tips and resources to educate yourself and your child about staying safe and behaving in a kind and ethical manner online. Because this is a book about electronic addiction, you might already assume that your child is at risk for falling prey to damaging experiences online. The information in *Parent's Quick Guide to Electronic Addiction* is not intended to provide all the training you need about online safety and addresses only the most pressing risks to your child at the time I wrote it. Be sure to continue to access new information after reading this book.

Cyberbullying

Cyberbullying is defined as someone under eighteen years of age tormenting, threatening, harassing, humiliating, or embarrassing someone else online who is under eighteen years of age. If one of the two parties involved is an adult, it's called cyber harassment or cyberstalking. (http://www.stopcyberbullying.org)

Cyberbullying can occur on social media sites such as Facebook, Snapchat, and Instagram; via text or instant message; and via email. There are apps such as Line and Sarahah that allow users to send messages, make calls, or text anonymously and then delete those messages. Cyberbullying can occur in a variety of ways, including:

- Posting or sharing lies, rumors, or private information
- Ridiculing someone about their personal appearance, school performance, clothing, socio-economic status, religion, or sexuality
- Threatening to harm or kill
- Encouraging suicide or self-harm
- Sharing nude or embarrassing photos or videos

Someone can unknowingly become a cyberbully by failing to think through their actions and posting an angry comment or an embarrassing photo of a peer. Others willfully set out to harm someone with a campaign of vicious attacks designed to bully a classmate. Unfortunately, cyberbullying is becoming more and more common, even leading to suicide. Recently there was a case of kids using Facebook Live to taunt another student to kill himself. Cyberbullying can have deadly consequences.

Cyberbullying is a worry for most kids. They are aware of it and fear it. Research conducted in 2016 found that 33.8 percent of students will experience cyberbullying, and 11.5 percent admitted to cyberbullying others. (http://enough.org/stats_cyberbullying)

Teach your child about cyberbullying by discussing things like:

- How would you feel if someone put a photo of you changing in gym class on Snapchat?
- Why do people feel safe saying things online that they would not say face to face?
- What should you do if someone sends you a message or text that is hurtful or threatening?
- What things are private and what can be shared online?
- Do you think people should ask permission before making or sharing videos of others?
- What should people do with photos of a former romantic partner after they break up?
- Have you ever seen someone try to hurt or shame someone online? What did you do about it?
- What would you do if someone sent you a nude photo?
- What would you do if someone tried to extort you [define this for them] about a photo they had of you?
- Do you know cyberbullying is illegal in some states? Where we live the law is _____.
  [Learn the law in your state. Ask your local school district for this information.]

Asking open-ended questions like these can help you teach your child about cyberbullying through conversations, which are always more effective than lectures. There are also some outstanding videos on YouTube about cyberbullying for elementary, middle school, and high school students. When I searched there today, there were almost half a million results. It's easy to find instructional videos appropriate for your child. Watch some of them together and then discuss them.

It is also important to teach your child about libel and slander. Some people post rumors or accusations about teachers, school administrators, employers, or coaches that can ruin lives, including the life of the person who posts them. Kids think it's funny to suggest that an adult likes pornography, drinks on the job, or is having an affair with a student. Young people believe that posting something like that is just a joke or a way to get back at someone. Be sure to discuss this issue with your child and the serious implications of such cyber harassment.

To learn more about cyberbullying, simply search the internet. Here are some sites to get you started:

- https://cyberbullying.org
- https://www.stopbullying.gov
- http://www.stopcyberbullying.org

Video and Photo Sharing

Matt Burk told me, "I tell my son that he is not in trouble if someone sends him risqué photos or videos, but he can be in trouble if he passes them on to others, as that can be considered engaging in child pornography." Unfortunately, there is little you can do to prevent your child from receiving explicit material, so teach them to tell you if they get such material and that you will help them take appropriate action. This is an excellent time to talk about how someone might feel if a photo of them was circulating at school without their permission. This discussion will help your child learn empathy by considering others, which is difficult for some kids to process.

I also recommend that you contact the parent of anyone who sends your child pornographic or inappropriate material. They probably have no idea and would appreciate the information, even if they initially deny it. No one wants to believe their darling child would do such a thing. If your child continues to receive inappropriate material and the other parent does not take any action to stop it, or their efforts fail, you might want to contact the police.

Predators and Sex Trafficking

The internet harbors a wide variety of nefarious adults who try to lure children into terrible situations. The average age at which a child enters the sex trade in the U.S. is from twelve to fourteen years old. (https://www.dosomething.org/us/facts/11-facts-about-human-trafficking)

It is imperative to teach your child to be watchful and to not put themselves in harm's way by revealing personal information, agreeing to meet, or believing that someone they have never met wants to date them or be their friend. Talk with them about how adults pose as teens to trick people into dangerous situations.

Again, YouTube has some terrific videos that can help you teach your child about online predators. There are thousands of videos aimed at all age groups. Search for the following terms:

- Social media safety
- Online safety
- Online predators

The process that predators use to lure kids is called grooming. If you notice any of the signs listed below, your child might have a problem with an internet predator:

- An increased amount of time spent online or on their phone
- Secrecy about sites visited or people they are in contact with
- Switching screens or hiding their phone or computer screen when you come into the room
- Using sexual language that does not match their age or your family values
- Anxiety or emotional volatility, especially when they're not able to connect electronically
- Calls, presents, mail, or contacts from people you don't know
- Having a phone or other electronic device that you did not supply

(https://internetsafety101.org/predatorwarningsigns)

The Dark Web

There are places online where you can buy drugs, weapons, or access child pornography. It's called the dark web, and it is not a place for our children to be visiting. This is where criminals, terrorists, and unsavory characters hang out. The dark web is not accessible via regular search engines like Google or Bing. Instead it is accessed via a downloadable program called The

Onion Network (TOR), which encrypts all the information there. If you see "TOR" or "The Onion Network" in your child's browsing history, they are most likely accessing the dark web.

Like anything forbidden, the dark web can be appealing to kids who want to see what is going on there. Talk to your child about the risks and dangers of the dark web. For more information visit https://securingtomorrow.mcafee.com/ consumer/family-safety/dark-web-what-every-parent-should-know.

CHAPTER 14

FOR OLDER TEENS: PORN, ONLINE DATING, AND COLLEGE TIPS

I had a client who was accused of inappropriate sexual activity with a partner. They had been consensually intimate many times and had engaged in oral sex. In the instance that resulted in the accusation, the partner claimed to be intoxicated and unconscious. When the partner accused my client of inappropriate sexual activity via text message, my client did not agree but wanted to preserve their relationship, and apologized via text. Now that text message is being used as evidence of guilt.

A young woman I know posted photos to her friends online of herself in suggestive poses and partying hard. She does not realize that these photos of her college experiences could cost her a job in the future. Employers check social media – wouldn't you?

Older teens and college students are at risk in the electronic world just as their younger and more innocent peers are. Just because your child is an older teen, don't assume they are fully aware of the impact of the internet.

Electronic Addiction and the Older Teen

Unfortunately, most people do not just grow out of electronic addiction as they become adults. I have clients who flunked out of college because they spent too much time with their electronics and did not attend classes or do homework; others were tethered to friends or romantic partners and spent hours sexting. Some students use their cell phones to take photos of tests and pass along the information to friends. I even know students who try to buy their term papers online.

Coming into adulthood is always challenging. The electronic world plays a big role in the challenges our older teens encounter. Here are tips for older students:

- Professors check for online plagiarism.
- Everyone thinks they won't get caught.
- Cheating is a very serious infraction.
- Others will turn you in to save themselves.
- Balanced electronic use is positive and helpful. Set a limit for your electronic use and do your best to stick to it.

Dating

Dating used to be a process of interacting with many people to find out what you like and need in a relationship, sorting through several people to find the one person you want to be with. Today's kids don't even have to date. They can go to Tinder.com and find someone to sleep with by just looking at their photo. Instead of a romantic relationship, they can have a "fuck buddy," a vile term in my opinion!

Many teens do not understand the difference between love and sex. They are led to believe that everyone else is having lots of great sex and that they are losers if they aren't. Because of the proliferation of and easy access to online porn and social media, kids develop unrealistic expectations about what real people look like and how they behave. In the online porn world, everyone is beautiful and wants to have mind-blowing sex immediately without any courtship or feelings involved. In the online world we post only our best photos or Photoshop them to look even better.

Teenagers can be anyone they want to be in the online world by hiding flaws and creating profiles completely different from their actual personality. They fall in love with a character, not a real person with strengths and challenges. The online world focuses on looks and easy interactions. Kids engage in sexual conversations and mutual masturbation with online strangers at the click of a mouse or a swipe of their cell phone. It seems easier than getting up the courage to go on a date, so no wonder they're attracted to it.

It might feel uncomfortable to talk with your older teen about sex and the electronic world, but it is a very important conversation. Talk about what love and romance are and contrast them with a one-night hookup. You don't need to discourage online dating, but discuss the difference between sites that focus on matching people with common interests and sites that promote spontaneous sexual activity. Point out the joy of seeing the natural beauty in others as opposed to the airbrushed images of celebrities, models, and film stars. What many adolescents miss is that relationships are not based just on looks. Teach your child that looks are just the outside packaging and that meaningful relationships are built on knowing a person, developing trust over time, and learning and growing together.

Sameer Hinduja, Ph.D., is a Fulbright scholar and co-founder of the Cyberbullying Research Center. He offers excellent information for older teens regarding online dating and sexting. He and Dr. Justin Patchin define sexting as "the sending or receiving of sexually-explicit or sexually-suggestive photos or video via cell phone." (https://cyberbullying.org/sexting-a-brief-guide-for-educators-and-parents-2)

It is important to talk with your teen about respecting their body and not treating it like a piece of meat. It can seem flirty, fun, and a common practice to send suggestive photos, but such photos can be passed on without permission. Discuss the potential shame and embarrassment this can cause as well as the legal implications of minors having those types of photos in their device histories. Ask them what kinds of relationships they lead to, and why they are searching for love in all the wrong places.

Encourage your child to be sure all photos and videos they share can be rated PG – something they would not mind their grandmother seeing. Tell them that if they receive explicit photos they should report them to you, and to never share them or pass them on to others.

This is a great opportunity to reinforce the idea of personal boundaries and talk about what your child can do if someone sends nude or sexually explicit material, especially if it's from a stranger or someone with whom they do not have a romantic relationship. Encourage them to block anyone who sends an inappropriate photo or video and to tell you if they ever feel threatened or sexually harassed online. There is a helpful factsheet that can aid your discussion at https://cyberbullying. org/sexting-advice-teens.

Phone Etiquette

Many teens have no idea how to manage their electronics while on a date. I'm sure you've seen couples sitting in restaurants not speaking but engrossed in their phones. If you see this with your child, it's a great opportunity for a discussion. Use these questions or similar ones to open a conversation:

- Do you think they're enjoying their date?
- Is it a good idea to have your phone on the table during a date?
- What would you think if someone checked their texts while on a date with you?
- What's the best way to handle an incoming phone call during a date?
- How would you feel if your date was glued to their phone instead of talking with you?
- Is there a way to use a phone to enhance a date? [Show photos of family, pets, and vacations. Share information about yourself and get to know each other. A shy person can use the technology on their cell phone as a conversation-starter.]

When you ask open-ended questions, asking your child for their opinion, you can have a much more fruitful discussion than if you just preach at them.

Career Implications

Remind your teen or young adult that everything online is searchable and part of the public record. Photos and videos of parties on spring break or that wild night at the club can be found by potential employers. It is common practice now for employers to do internet searches and review social media sites and online photos to access the character of candidates for employment. Once posted, they can always be found. Deleted information is retrievable if you know how.

This issue is complicated by the fact that kids can film others and post those pictures and videos online, tagging them by name, without asking. A roommate or even a stranger at a party can post something very incriminating, especially if illegal substances are involved. Everyone around us has a video camera, not to mention the presence of surveillance cameras.

Remind your child that anything online or on a cell phone can be retrieved by the police as evidence. Tell them about employment online searches. Advise them to talk with their friends and agree to never post photos of each other without permission. They should also talk about watching out for each other by alerting friends if they see any compromising photos or videos online.

It would be great to think that our kids will never do anything that should not be viewed online. But kids make mistakes; it's part of growing up. Inform them of the consequences of airing those mistakes online. (It makes those of older generations glad that there were no cell phone cameras when we were in college!)

A Positive Use of Electronics

Parents of college students need to be careful about keeping their kids too tethered to home. I have known parents of clients who text their college students multiple times each day and then become frustrated when their texts are ignored. It is okay to check in with your college student, but use a balanced approach.

If your child struggles with time management or electronic addiction when away at school, use your electronic devices proactively. Have your child send you a photo of themselves entering the building of their early morning class or studying at the library. That seems invasive to most students, but if your child struggles to balance electronics use, sending photos is an excellent way to help them learn to be responsible, especially during their first semester away from home or if they're having trouble with their schoolwork. Have them set alarms to text you updates about how they're doing. College costs a lot. Be proactive!

CHAPTER 15

HOW TO FIND HELP IF YOU SUSPECT ELECTRONIC ADDICTION

If you suspect that your child has an electronic addiction, getting the right kind of professional support is very important. Remember our definition of electronic addiction from the beginning of this book: it creates problems in daily life. Kids with this challenge continue to use electronics even after negative consequences.

Parents are sometimes unsure of what kind of help to pursue. They might start with their pediatrician or a psychiatrist. I recommend beginning instead with a licensed therapist who is trained in specific techniques for working with kids with electronic addiction. If the therapist uncovers a medical issue or potential need for medication, they can help you find a physician to add to the treatment team. My rule of thumb is that pills without skills will not solve the problem.

Consider therapy for your child, and parent coaching for your own personal support. Therapy involves specific assessment and treatment of mental health conditions.

Coaching provides intervention ideas to help solve a problem. Parent coaching can be very helpful even if you don't have your child assessed for mental health issues and potential treatment. It can also be beneficial to join a support network with other parents to share ideas about helping children overcome electronic addiction.

(Parent coaching is such an important element in managing a child with electronic addiction that I offer webinars and other trainings for clinicians who want experience in this emerging field. There is more information at the back of this book and on my website, including a list of therapists who have completed the training. Visit http://CenterForElectronicAddiction.com.)

In the city where I work, people say, "If therapy doesn't work, try Dr. Berk." I have always loved working with kids who have behavioral challenges. When I was in high school I got a job at the YMCA and was always assigned the kids no one else could work with. I liked them and wanted to find out how to help them, which led to my doctorate degree in psychology and a twenty-five-year career as a child therapist.

One of the most significant problems I encounter is that parents wait too long to initiate therapy when they suspect an electronic addiction or other mental health concern. You might think you know your child better than anyone else, but if your child is struggling, start therapy as soon as possible. The longer addictive behavior continues, the more entrenched it becomes.

Your first step is to talk with your child's school counselor about your concerns to find out if teachers or school personnel have noticed failing grades, unusual behavior, or social isolation.

Ask for referrals to qualified therapists who have experience with electronic addiction.

Because this is a new problem, it can be challenging to find a therapist in your local area who has this level of expertise. If there is no one in your community with experience in electronic addiction, look for a psychologist who treats other addictions in young people using cognitive behavioral therapy, which focuses on helping people learn about their thinking and behavior so that they can make positive changes. I find it very useful for helping kids of all ages.

Finding a good therapist for your child takes some time and research. Ask other parents for referrals. Once you have identified some potential therapists, meet with them and show them your copy of this book to demonstrate that you have done your homework and to see if they are familiar with the strategies I suggest and can take you and your child to next steps. Ask if they have any experience treating individuals with electronic addiction. Go on introductory visits with your child. It's important to find a therapist who establishes rapport with you and your child. If your child is already in therapy for another issue, talk with the therapist about your concerns and find out if they have experience with electronic addiction.

Most therapists who work with addictions offer individual therapy, family therapy, and group programs to support recovery. That is the approach I use in my office. I treat the individual in private sessions, have some sessions with the young person and their parent or parents, and recommend a social-skills group. Social issues are almost always a related problem.

Social-skills training is a vital part of a treatment plan for electronic addiction. As you remember from chapter 10, most kids who have an electronic addiction have deficits in social skills. The best way for them to learn social skills is in a group setting with others at their developmental stage. My recommendation is that groups have around ten participants with similarities in age, developmental stage, and challenge. For example, I offer social-skills training for kids with ADHD separately from those with depression so that each group is tailored to the unique characteristics of the participants.

Ask the therapists you are vetting if they provide all three types of services: individual; family, or parent-and-child; and social-skills groups. Be sure to get references even if you have been referred by someone you trust, *and call the references*; you might find out something that the person who referred you doesn't know about. Use these questions to complete your research about social-skills groups:

- How many kids are in each group?
- What structure does the group follow?
- Is the purpose of the group to talk about feelings or to develop skills?
- How do you group the participants?
- Will group activities be part of my child's treatment plan?
- How will I know what my child is learning about in group therapy so I can reinforce it at home?
- Will my child have their own goal for therapy beyond that of the group?

Talking to Your Child about Therapy

It can be hard to talk to your child about starting treatment for their electronic addiction. I recommend an honest and caring approach. Say something like "I am concerned about how much time you are spending online and the fact that you are [losing friends, having trouble at school, etc.]. I'd like for us to go together to Dr. X and see what we can do to help." Ask your child to think about these questions:

- What am I missing because of my use of electronics?
- Have I harmed anyone or anything because I want to be online?
- Do I get angry when I must stop gaming or stop using my phone?
- Have I stopped doing something I used to enjoy to focus on things that are online?
- Has anyone told me I use electronics too much?
- Have I lost friends because I am online a lot?

Discuss what they are missing by not having friends and a social life. Some kids have no idea what they are missing. They say they are happy in their isolation because they haven't experienced lasting friendships and enjoyable social interactions.

Therapy should not be seen as punishment. Don't say things like "If you don't quit that, I'm going to tell Dr. X." Instead, stress that working with a therapist will help them learn to use electronics in a balanced way so that they can be online and still have a great life offline.

Remind your child that when they have a health issue like bronchitis or a broken leg, they go to a professional for treatment; that seeing a therapist doesn't mean they are crazy or broken, it just means that they have thoughts or behaviors that are causing them problems and that getting treatment for those challenges is smart and just as important as seeing a physician for a physical illness or injury.

Stress that therapy is private, and no one needs to know about it unless your child wants to share the information. Because kids feel social pressure, they don't want to be teased or be a topic of gossip at school. Stressing confidentiality will help allay those fears.

Suicide

Never take threats of suicide or your own suspicions of the potential of suicide lightly. Kids say things like "If you make me go to a therapist, I'm going to kill myself." This can be an idle threat, but it can also be a serious intention. To ensure the safety of your child, take any mention of suicide seriously and go immediately for an evaluation. If they post such information, take it seriously! Wrong once is too many times. If your child says a friend posted something suicidal, call that parent! Think how you would feel if you didn't and their child carried out their threat.

Common signs of suicidal intentions in kids include:

- Talking about suicide or plans for it
- Hopelessness
- Symptoms of deep emotional pain
- Changes in behavior including sleep patterns, loss of appetite, uncharacteristic hostility, aggression, and irritability
- Giving away treasured possessions

- Lack of interest in school, falling grades, and undone homework
- Drawing pictures related to death
- Isolation
- Joking or making statements about death, suicide, or not being around any longer
- Withdrawal or extreme boredom
- Changes in personality
- Drug or alcohol use

It's weird, but true, that those who have decided to kill themselves can become quite calm and stop exhibiting the signs listed above because they are no longer in the throes of making the decision – they are now content and comfortable with the decision. This is the time of highest risk. You can observe this change because it happens suddenly once the decision is made, rather than gradually.

If you see any of these signs in your child, get immediate help. If your child threatens suicide or you suspect that they are considering it, go immediately to the nearest emergency room. Tell them, "I'm concerned that you might hurt yourself and I want to go with you to get some help." If your child will not go with you, call 911. Doing so involves the police and escalates the situation, but if that is your only recourse, make the call. It is better to be wrong about the situation than to ignore something that could contribute to your child's death.

If you have guns in your home, be sure they are in a locked gun safe with ammunition stored in a different locked area. Also ensure that medications, alcohol, and even bottles of aspirin are securely stored out of reach.

These tips are not solutions, just precautions; and taking precautions is not a substitute for medical care and therapy.

Signs of a Positive Relationship with a Therapist

It is important that your child's therapist develops a treatment plan and shares it with you and your child. There are boundary and privacy issues in therapy. The therapist will meet privately with your child, but most will also meet with you to ensure that you have the resources you need at home to support the treatment plan they established. You might meet privately with the therapist and have joint sessions with the therapist and your child.

Electronic addiction is a challenging problem and requires time and a united effort of many adults to cure. However, it is very possible to help kids learn to use electronics in a healthy and balanced manner, so don't give up if it seems difficult or your child has a setback.

Please do not stop therapy too soon. It's not the time to quit when you see success; you want to reinforce that success! I have known parents who put an end to their child's therapy sessions prematurely, leading to a relapse. It takes long-term support for your child to learn how to manage their behavior and emotions independently. There will be a time when their therapist's support is no longer required, but you should make the decision to discontinue therapy in collaboration with the therapist and your child.

If Therapy Is Not Working

Not every therapist can successfully treat every kid. Sometimes personalities just don't mesh, or progress plateaus.

If you don't observe signs of improvement after three to six months of therapy, talk with the therapist about getting a second opinion. An ethical professional will welcome this kind of conversation and might be able to recommend a therapist more suited to your child's temperament. If they don't, go back to the drawing board and seek out someone else.

CHAPTER 16

ADDRESSING A RELAPSE

Some kids make great strides in curbing their electronic addiction and then have a relapse. This is understandable and to be expected. Just as with other addictions, cravings to use electronics in an addictive way are very strong, especially for young people.

Think of the electronic world as your child's security blanket. It seems safe, secure, and offers the comfort of the familiar. When kids are stressed it can be very tempting to withdraw into the electronic world. I have a theory I call "predictive crappiness." This means that someone would rather stay in a bad situation that is familiar, such as electronic addiction, than risk trying something new that might fail. Your child might know that staying up all night gaming or spending hours on their phone is unhealthy, but they would rather stick with the familiar than try a new activity or friendship.

Your child can relapse after cessation of electronic addiction if they encounter an emotional challenge such as:

- A breakup with a girlfriend or boyfriend
- Loss of a close friendship
- Bullying

- Failure in school or a social context
- Loss of a part-time job
- Apprehension about testing for college, attending college, or entering the workforce

If you suspect a return to electronic addiction, remain calm. Relapses are part of recovery. They provide your child with the opportunity to learn from their mistakes and recover after a setback.

Characterize the situation as a learning opportunity, using a collaborative, problem-solving approach instead of punishing or demeaning your child. Instead of saying something negative like "I am so disappointed in you. I spent all that money on therapy and you are still hiding in your room playing those dumb games," use a more supportive approach: Say, "I'm noticing a few things that make me wonder if you are having trouble balancing your screen time. Let's talk about it."

Many young people cannot express their feelings, especially when they are overwhelmed. Ask gently probing questions such as:

- You've really been under a lot of pressure lately. How are you feeling?
- I know that you and your [girlfriend or boyfriend] just broke up. That's really hard. How are you doing?
- I haven't seen your friend Taylor around lately. Are you guys okay?
- You are spending a lot more time alone in your room lately. Is everything alright?

These kinds of open-ended questions can encourage your child to talk with you. Have these conversations in a neutral environment that fosters communication. Remember that I suggested doughnut shops earlier in the book? Taking your child out for breakfast or a snack, traveling in the car, or sitting in the backyard together can set the stage for a collaborative conversation instead of a painful confrontation.

If your child is seeing a therapist and agrees that electronics are becoming a problem again, suggest that they bring it up in their next therapy appointment. If the problem is more imminent, offer to call and set up an appointment as soon as possible. It is best for your child to discuss the relapse with their therapist, but if they are unwilling or unable to do so, ask for their permission to bring it up with the therapist. Say something like, "Would you like to discuss this with Dr. X or should I let him know you are struggling?" Also suggest natural supports like friends, coaches, and teachers who can help. Say, "You always enjoy spending time with Jill. How about inviting her over this weekend?"

Holistic Intervention

Whether you've tackled your child's electronic addiction on your own or enlisted the help of a therapist, if you sense your child is struggling with a relapse, remember to consider all the facets of their life discussed above – known as a holistic approach – to see if you can pinpoint the source of the current stressor. These include:

- Nutrition
- Exercise
- Academic struggles: Many people have processing problems or other learning disabilities that don't become clear until middle school or high school. If your child is not able to perform well at school, request an evaluation.

- Friendships: Is your child losing friends or connecting with people who are leading them down a dark path?
- Check their browsing history. If they are searching for information on suicide, violence, or self-harm, there is a problem that requires intervention.
- An inability to feel happy or enjoy things. (A therapist might refer to this as *anhedonia*.)
- Change of friends

If your child has gone through a traumatic event, it is understandable that they would turn back to the electronic world for comfort or respite. Discuss this with them and say, "I know you are hurting because Jamie dumped you and that being online feels safe. It's okay if you need to retreat for a few more days, but if this goes on longer than a week, it might be a sign of a problem." Setting a time limit for recovery can be an excellent way to let your child process what happened but not get sucked back into an addictive pattern.

After you have considered all possible stressors, suggest small changes that don't feel overwhelming or scary, such as bike riding or other outdoor activities, joining a low-risk club at school, volunteering, and getting more sleep. If your child is seeing a therapist, communicate with the therapist to choose strategies that complement the supports provided by them. Work together to help your child get back on track.

Creating a Relapse Prevention Plan

Since your child has already been through a process of addressing their electronic addiction by adhering to the intervention plan, they can now work with you to generate a plan to address their relapse. Their therapist should help with this if your child is seeing one. I suggest some joint meetings with you, your child, and their therapist to create this plan. Here are some questions for your child to consider:

- Where do I use electronics the most?
- Which devices am I most susceptible to overusing?
- When do I tend to overuse electronics?
- Who encourages me to overuse electronics?
- What feelings trigger me to overuse electronics?
- What will I do instead when I have these feelings? Am I going to call somebody? How will I get help?
- It's easy to tell myself that I will get online for only a short while and then forget to cut it short. How will I time myself to prevent this?

Suggest that your child find some new leisure activities to occupy their time and prevent returning to an overuse of electronics caused by boredom. They can try a new hobby; work out with a partner; go fishing, biking, skating, hiking, or swimming; get a part-time job; or become active in a volunteer or religious organization. Add in more fun family activities. If you can encourage your child to fill their time with fun activities with others, they will have less time to retreat into electronics.

Your child might need a sponsor – someone who will help them stick with their affirmative plans and provide support when they are tempted to return to old patterns. It is not as easy to find a sponsor for an electronic addiction as it is for a substance abuse problem, but there might be a trusted adult, friend, cousin, or youth leader who is willing to fill this role.

The bottom line is that relapsing will likely occur. It is an expected part of the recovery process. When it happens for your child, and it will, the best option is to stay calm, talk about it, and develop a plan with your child (and their therapist if they're seeing one) to return to healthy electronics use and maintain a balance in the future.

Your child will be disappointed in themselves and ashamed by the relapse, even if they don't admit it. By not punishing but using collaborative problem-solving, you'll help make the recovery process smoother. It is an opportunity for your child to learn to recover from failure themselves and move on in a positive direction. That is a valuable life skill.

CHAPTER 17

SUMMARY

Congratulations! You are near the end of *Parent's Quick Guide to Electronic Addiction* and are now equipped with a deeper understanding of electronic addiction as well as some tools to help you either prevent it or start the process of helping your child overcome it.

Even if your child does not yet show signs of addiction, create a family electronic landscape to set the stage for their electronics use throughout their formative years. At the very least it will make your child aware of the risks and teach them self-management. To that end I've created some useful checklists for you. Choose the one that best suits your situation and follow the steps outlined. If you would like a free downloadable copy of these checklists, visit http://CenterForElectronicAddiction.com.

Checklist #1: Identification of an electronic addiction

- Does your child exhibit any of these signs of potential electronic addiction?
  - o Isolation
  - o Irritability
  - o Money-seeking

- o Relationship changes
- o Accessing adult websites
- o No desire to participate in typical activities for kids their age
- o Loss of friend-friends
- o Aggression
- o Poor choice of peer groups
- o Inability to balance screen time with other activities
- Has anyone suggested that your child overuses electronics?
- Does your child have any of these conditions that can exacerbate developing an electronic addiction?
  - o A mental health challenge
  - o A history of any type of addiction in your family
  - o A developmental disorder or a learning disability
- Do you feel uncomfortable with how much time your child spends on electronics?
- Is your child a loner or do they avoid engaging in friendships with peers from school or the neighborhood?
- Does your child prefer electronics over sports, hobbies, or time with others?
- Does your child explode or refuse when you request that they stop using electronics?
- Are you arguing with your child about their electronics use?
- Is your child having trouble at school with either academics or getting along with others?
- Do others bully or dislike your child?
- Is it a challenge for your child to interact with peers and/ or adults?

- Do you suspect that your child is accessing inappropriate, dark, or sexually explicit materials?

The more yeses, the more likely that your child has an electronic addiction, so begin using the strategies in this book.

Checklist #2: Prevention Practices

- Encourage your child to participate in hobbies, sports, and community or volunteer activities.
- Spend time as a family doing activities that do not involve electronics such as hiking; camping; attending sporting events, plays, or concerts; participating in religious or community activities; bowling, skating, or even playing arcade games; and pursing hobbies together.
- Get a pet that your child will want to help take care of.
- Encourage your child to volunteer at an animal shelter or rescue center. Shy kids often feel more comfortable around animals than they do around people.
- Encourage your child to research places of interest and routes for family vacations and outings.
- For young children, limit exposure to electronic devices and don't use them as time-fillers.
- Be sure your child gets plenty of quality sleep, exercise, and healthy foods.
- Create your family electronic landscape with your child, covering how and when electronics will be used.
- Set up parental controls on cell phones, computers, and gaming systems.
- Monitor your child's online activity regularly.

- Educate your child about internet safety and ethics. Make discussions about electronic security part of regular family talks.
- Find age-appropriate educational videos on YouTube, social media, and other media, and view them together.
- Teach your child how to identify safe sites, and fake news and postings.
- Include in your electronic landscape what kinds of photos and family information can and cannot be shared online.
- Foster social-skills development by arranging play dates or activities with friends, teaching about the differences between online and real-world friends.
- Support your child's academic success. Talk to school personnel if you sense a learning or developmental problem.
- Watch movies as a family about bullying, childhood friendships, and other developmental topics, and discuss them.
- Have regular family game nights.

Checklist #3: Intervention Strategies

- Start with all the prevention practices in list #2 above.
- Review your family electronic landscape and develop an intervention plan with your child.
- Discuss your concerns with a school counselor to determine if problems are showing up at school.
- Ask for therapist referrals from school personnel and other parents.
- Vet therapists to ensure they have experience with electronic addiction or are willing to learn more about it.

- Attend therapy with your child.
- Find appropriate social-skills training.
- Talk about your concerns with your child.
- Get all adults – parents, step-parents, and grandparents – involved in the plan.
- Start with the Pay to Play system.
- Use Amish Paradise sparingly as a consequence for not meeting expectations.
- Watch for signs of relapse.
- Treat relapses as learning opportunities.
- Always maintain a supportive and collaborative approach, talking with your child about how to solve the problem together.
- Be prepared to address this challenge for as long as needed to ensure your child has mastered it. Let them continue in therapy until all parties agree it is no longer needed.
- Contact Dr. Berk for parent coaching.

Thank you for caring enough about your child to read about how to address the problem of electronic addiction. You are investing in a better future for your child!

A NOTE FROM THE AUTHOR

I trust *Parent's Quick Guide to Electronic Addiction* has given you much to think about and practical ideas you can use in your family. Will you help me spread the word about the challenge of electronic addiction? You can do so by going to Amazon.com and posting an honest review about this book, whether you purchased it from Amazon or not. Book reviews help books get more attention in the search traffic on Amazon, so by leaving a review you are helping more parents obtain this important information. Simply go to Amazon and enter the title of the book in the search bar, then scroll down the page until you see the "Write a Customer Review" button.

Please share this book with other parents, therapists, and educators. I'm on a mission to help families combat electronic addiction, so the more people who have this information, the easier it will be for us to work together to help our kids learn to use electronics in a healthy and balanced way.

All my best to you and your family,

Dr. Jay Berk

ABOUT THE AUTHOR

Dr. Jay H. Berk is a licensed psychologist in two U.S. states and an expert in working with children, adolescents, and families. He also conducts social-skills groups for children and adolescents. In addition to providing therapy, he is a guest lecturer throughout the world and provides training and workshops throughout the U.S. and abroad to schools, agencies, and a variety of groups. In his private practice he conducts therapy with children, adolescents, adults, families, and couples.

Dr. Berk functions as a special consultant to the Screen Actors Guild – American Federation of Television and Radio Artists (SAG-AFTRA) in New York City on an ongoing basis and provides many seminars each year for parents and young performers. He was a consultant to the United Nations Children's Fund (UNICEF) and wrote a manual for UNICEF used by teachers to work with children in Bosnia during the Bosnian War. He has lectured at the Royal Brisbane Hospital in Queensland, Australia; the Royal Children's Hospital in Melbourne, Australia; the University of London; the Cleveland Clinic; the Disney Channel; SAG-AFTRA; the Young Professionals Organization; and many school districts and universities throughout the U.S.

Dr. Berk is adept at treating children and adolescents in outpatient and residential programs. His experience includes working at several children's homes. In addition to electronic addiction, his specialties include clients with stress and anxiety, social issues, obsessive compulsive disorder, learning disabilities, attention deficit disorder, autism, developmental disorders (including those formerly diagnosed as Asperger's syndrome, now called social communication disorder), and Tourette's syndrome, and he treats clients who have multiple impairments. He is also an expert in working with oppositional defiant children and adolescents and their families.

Dr. Berk works with young performers with issues related to stage and screen success, including teamwork with other performers; and with other high-profile children and families to help them cope with the unique pressures of this lifestyle. His practice is held in high regard in the performing arts industry and provides a spectrum of interventions for these individuals, their families, and personnel who work with them.

Dr. Berk served as a special consultant to businesses, schools, and other private organizations in the areas of employee relations, employee assistance programs, policy setting, and reducing burnout. He instructed paramedics in field management of behavioral emergencies. He served as a member of, and trainer for, the Greater Cleveland Chapter of the American Red Cross Disaster Mental Health team and responded to emergencies such as air disasters and fires where there was loss of life. He provided training in debriefing and trauma-response for clinicians and emergency responders and was responsible for debriefing personnel from the American Red Cross–Cleveland Chapter who provided relief services to hurricane sites. He developed a plan to "Help the Helpers," an overall program for training responders, providing more effective services onsite and facilitating smooth reintegration of disaster volunteers into the workplace upon their return from a disaster.

Also especially notable is that Dr. Berk provided the keynote address at the University of Arkansas–Jonesboro seminar following the school shooting that occurred there. He currently facilitates several social-skills groups for people from ages three to thirty-five. He is available to speak privately to groups of any size and contracts with businesses, seminar companies, schools, and universities to provide in-service training.

ACKNOWLEDGMENTS

First and foremost, I would like to acknowledge the support of my loving, caring wife, partner, and best friend, Kelly Vitello. Kelly has been at my side supporting me as a professional for many years and has been a great mother, a professional in her own right, and my biggest fan.

I would like to thank my children, Chapin and Mackenzie, for their help. Parents just can't overestimate the love they feel for their children. The moment they are born this love magically happens. My children have taken me on a journey that has had many ups and downs. They have taught me how to speak in words that teenagers use nowadays and tell me I'm old when I use terms from my childhood. Without their contributions, this book would not exist.

I would like to thank all the thousands of people who attended seminars I presented over the past twenty years on topics such as social skills, autism, mental health in the schools, oppositional defiant children, and electronic addiction. Interacting with them has been and continues to be illuminating. As a clinician who also teaches, they help me stay up to date on information. I've had many lively discussions during presentations with well-educated attendees who provided stimulating and enriching conversation for not just myself but the other participants as well.

I thank all my clients who have trusted me with their care. I primarily treat children and adolescents, but now treat adults as well, especially since many of the kids I have worked with are now adults. (Amazing how that happens.) I learn from them as they learn from me, and that sharing experience helps them grow in their mental health.

My practice would be nothing without the support I receive from clinicians and the staff members in my office. At Jay Berk, Ph.D. & Associates we have two support staff members at our Beachwood, Ohio, location, Kathleen and Marianne, who have made the office what it is. From the moment someone contacts us they receive care, concern, and warm engagement that they experience nowhere else, and that makes them want to come see us.

I would like to thank my best friend, companion, and colleague for over forty years, Joe Priore. Who has a friendship that lasts forty years? I am fortunate to have one. In terms of advocacy and cheerleading, he has been my biggest supporter. I started working at the YMCA forty years ago with children no one else wanted to work with. He cheered me on, supported me, and told me to go out and achieve, and without Joe I don't think I would be where I am now.

I thank my parents, who are no longer alive but are still part of me. My father taught me a strong work ethic, dedication, and to believe in myself. After many years I was able to finish high school, a bachelor's degree, a master's degree, and a doctorate, and I was the first in my family to do so. My father supported me emotionally and financially through this process. My mother provided insight to help me go out and get what I wanted. There was no holding back in their encouragement of my efforts. If I believed I could do something, I would try it knowing I had their support.

My Aunt Mel and Uncle Gary also greatly supported me, and I thank them as well. They took me in when I was emotionally destitute and allowed me to use their home to find peace and reboot myself when I was down. Aunt Mel diligently called me, weekly sometimes, to provide emotional support during a very rough time in my life. They are the kind of relatives that you truly care about and who care about you. Thank you, Aunt Ray, Great-Aunt Stella, Great-Aunt Ruthie, Uncle Al, Aunt Eileen, Cousin Richie, and the rest of the clan. Although I did not see them as often as I would have liked, and they have passed away now, they each brought something special to my life. From them I learned hard work, dedication, to believe in myself, and to live a simple life and enjoy what you have.

ABOUT THE CENTER FOR ELECTRONIC ADDICTION

The Center for Electronic Addiction was founded in 2017 by Jay Berk, Ph.D., psychologist, speaker, clinician, and advocate. After many years of observing clients and working with children, adolescents, and young adults, it became obvious to him that there was a new phenomenon called electronic addiction. Although the *Diagnostic and Statistical Manual of Mental Disorders* (*DSM–5*) failed to recognize this and missed the mark in examining a condition called electronic gaming addiction, Dr. Berk believes firmly that there should be a diagnosis of electronic addiction in the next revision of the manual.

It is important that there be a diagnosis, collaborative care standards, and recognition by clinicians of electronic addiction so that insurance companies can cover treatment for those suffering from it. Most people with electronic addiction come to Jay Berk, Ph.D. & Associates with diagnoses such as depression, anxiety, social anxiety, autism, and symptoms related to these conditions that connect with electronic addiction.

As with more commonly recognized forms of addiction such as drug addiction, people realize the impact the addiction has in their life too late to avoid losing friendships, relationships, and jobs, and experience legal and other problems that could have been prevented had they been diagnosed earlier. Children and adolescents, especially, do not see it coming.

They are growing up in a world in which electronic addiction is so common that it is woven into the fabric of their lives. The purpose of the Center for Electronic Addiction is to:

1. Provide information to children, adolescents, adults, and families about recognizing the signs of addiction

2. Provide intervention and treatment strategies for those suffering from electronic addiction

3. Disseminate information to other clinicians about the diagnosis of electronic addiction and treatment modalities

4. Continue the pursuit of research and education about electronic addiction

5. Work toward qualifying electronic addiction as a diagnosis so that mental health clinicians can recognize and treat it effectively

6. Reduce stress in families in which someone suffers from electronic addiction

For more about the Center for Electronic Addiction, find them on the web at http://CenterforElectronicAddiction.com. They provide training, consultation, podcasts, and reading materials, and are developing more and more resources about this challenge. Jay Berk, Ph.D., is the director of the Center for Electronic Addiction and has over twenty-five years of experience working with children, adolescents, adults, and families, and has treated a wealth of cases of electronic addiction in this new and emerging field. You can join our newsletter and like us on Facebook. The information available about electronic addiction is increasing on a daily, weekly, monthly, and yearly basis, so keep in touch!

INDEX

Made in the USA
Lexington, KY
09 May 2018